SAP/ABAP HANA
PROGRAMMING

by

Sudipta Malakar

BPB PUBLICATIONS

20 Ansari Road, Darya Ganj New Delhi-110002

FIRST EDITION 2018

Copyright © BPB Publications, INDIA

ISBN: 978-93-8728-428-9

All Rights Reserved. No part of this publication can be stored in a retrieval system or reproduced in any form or by any means without the prior written permission of the publishers.

LIMITS OF LIABILITY AND DISCLAIMER OF WARRANTY

The Author and Publisher of this book have tried their best to ensure that the programmes, procedures and functions described in the book are correct. However, the author and the publishers make no warranty of any kind, expressed or implied, with regard to these programmes or the documentation contained in the book. The author and publisher shall not be liable in any event of any damages, incidental or consequential, in connection with, or arising out of the furnishing, performance or use of these programmes, procedures and functions. Product name mentioned are used for identification purposes only and may be trademarks of their respective companies.

All trademarks referred to in the book are acknowledged as properties of their respective owners.

Distributors:

BPB PUBLICATIONS
20, Ansari Road, Darya Ganj
New Delhi-110002
Ph: 23254990/23254991

BPB BOOK CENTRE
376 Old Lajpat Rai Market,
Delhi-110006
Ph: 23861747

DECCAN AGENCIES
4-3-329, Bank Street,
Hyderabad-500195
Ph: 24756967/24756400

MICRO MEDIA
Shop No. 5, Mahendra Chambers, 150
DN Rd. Next to Capital Cinema, V.T.
(C.S.T.) Station, MUMBAI-400 001 Ph:
22078296/22078297

COMPUTER BOOK CENTRE
12, Shrungar Shopping Centre,
M.G.Road, BENGALURU—560001
Ph: 25587923/25584641

Published by Manish Jain for BPB Publications, 20, Ansari Road, Darya Ganj, New Delhi-110002 and Printed by Repro India Ltd., Mumbai

Acknowledgement

No task is a single man's effort. Cooperation and Coordination of various peoples at different levels go into successful implementation of this book.

There is always a sense of gratitude, which every one expresses others for their helpful and needly services they render during difficult phases of life and to achieve the goal already set.

At the outset I am thankful to the almighty that is constantly and invisibly guiding every body and have also helped me to work on the right path.

I am very much thankful to **my parents, spouse, son and family** for their guidance which motivated me to work for the betterment of consultants by writing the book with sincerity and honesty. Without their support, this book is not possible.

I wish my sincere thanks to colleagues who helped and kept me motivated for writing this text.

We also thank the Publisher and the whole staff at **BPB Publications**, especially **Mr. Manish Jain** for motivation and for bringing this text in a nice presentable form.

Finally, I thank everyone who has directly or indirectly contributed to complete this authentic work.

Preface

SAP HANA (High-Performance Analytical Appliance) is an in-memory database engine from SAP that is used to analyze large data sets in real time that reside entirely in memory. Very crudely it is a Database System which totally changes the DBMS methodology and it can be deployable on premises or over cloud.

Notice how SAP HANA has changed the world now. Whether you are a newbie or an old-hat, you can learn to design & build simple and advanced SAP HANA applications with ABAP/4 by using this comprehensive artifact. You can also enrich your skill sets with the use of new Open SQL enhancements and CD5 views, and integrate native SAP HANA objects. Use this detailed programming referral guide to develop database procedures and optimize your applications. You'll be programming for SAP HANA in no time. The goal of writing this book is to describe different SAP ABAP programming best practices, taken reference from different SAP & IBM blogs, books, articles, Global networks, organizational forums, portals, wiki etc..

The Power of HANA

- ✓ Give business users the power to investigate and visualize their data with advanced analytic tools.
- ✓ Power applications that deliver real-time insights to drive more effective and timely decision making.
- ✓ Accelerate analytics, business processes, data processing, and predictive capabilities to run business in real-time.
- ✓ Quickly setup, deploy, and build real-time applications that feature mobile, collaboration, big data, and analytics services.

Capabilities	Customer Value
Columnar data storage	Data Compression
In-memory storage	Faster Aggregation
In-memory computation	Faster Calculation time
Integration with live replication	Real time analytics
No pre-aggregated tables	Simpler BI modelling
Direct usage of predictive functionality	Plug & Play

HANA Goals

- ✓ Enables New Application and Optimize Existing Application
- ✓ High Performance and Scalability
- ✓ **Hybrid Data** Management System
- ✓ Compatible with Standard DBMS feature
- ✓ Support for Text analysis, indexing and search
- ✓ **Cloud support** and application isolation
- ✓ Executing application logic inside the data layer

This book promises to be a very good starting point for beginners and an asset for those having insight towards programming.

It is said **"To err is human, to forgive divine"**. Although the book is written with sincerity and honesty but in this light author wish that the shortcomings of the book will be forgiven. At the same the author is open to any kind of constructive criticisms and suggestions for further improvement. All intelligent suggestions are welcome and the author will its their best to incorporate such in valuable suggestions in the subsequent editions of this book.

Table of Contents

CHAPTER 1

Introduction

Notice how SAP HANA has changed the world now. Whether you are a newbie or an old-hat, you can learn to design & build simple and advanced SAP HANA applications with ABAP/4 by using this comprehensive artifact. You can also enrich your skillsets with the use of new Open SQL enhancements and CD5 views, and integrate native SAP HANA objects. Use this detailed programming referral guide to develop database procedures and optimize your applications. You'll be programming for SAP HANA in no time.

Readers may enhance their skillsets with numerous buzzwords currently being used in IT organizations worldwide , like SAP HANA, SAP screen personas, SAP Fiori, ABAP, SAP HANA tables and their advantages over conventional tables, SQL, AMDP, CDS views on HANA, DML/DDL/DCL etc.

Target audience for this book may be in IT domain having software background, preferably with SAP technical or techno functional or functional or domain knowledge.

This book will teach you the basics of SAP HANA. The book is divided into sections such as SAP HANA Basics, SAP HANA-Modeling, Reporting, SAP HANA-SQL and case studies.

1.1   HANA Overview

What is HANA - SAP HANA (High-Performance Analytical Appliance) is an in-memory database engine from SAP that is used to analyze large data sets in real time that reside entirely in memory. Very crudely it is a Database System which totally changes the DBMS methodology and it can be deployable on premises or over cloud.

What is new in HANA – HANA is the first system to let you to perform real-time online application processing (OLAP) analysis on an online transaction processing (OLTP) data structure. As a result, you can address today's demand for real-time business insights by creating business applications that previously were neither feasible nor cost-effective.

SAP S/4HANA
Evolution

SAP S/4HANA, on-premise edition 1511

- Industry to core
  - Discrete Industries and Mill Products (DIMP)
- Effective Order Management and Billing
- Efficient Procurement
- Accelerated Material Requirements Planning
- Real-time Inventory Management and Material Valuation

SAP S/4HANA 1610

- Oil and Gas with SAP S/4HANA
- Industry to core – Retail
- Consistent SAP Fiori User Experience
- Optimized Portfolio and Project Management
- Embedded Software in Product Development
- Entire SAP S/4HANA Finance Scope included
- Plan to Produce in ONE System (Production Planning and Detailed Scheduling – PP/DS)
- Embedded SAP Extended Warehouse Management
- Integrated Quality Management
- advanced Available to Promise (aATP)

SAP S/4HANA 1709

- Industries to Core – SAP Agricultural Contract Management
- SAP Commercial Project Management with S/4HANA
- Commodity Management
- Sales – Electronic and Digital Payments
- GRC – Legal Control and Export Classification
- Consumer Products – Catch Weight Management
- SAP S/4HANA Central Master Data
- Finance – Machine Learning for automation capability
- QM – Manage usage decisions and Analytics for Quantitative Results
- EAM – Report and Repair Malfunction
- PLM – Visual Manufacturing Planner and Recipe Management
- Maximize Fiori Experience with SAP Fiori Overview Pages
- Predictive Analytics as a system of intelligence – Contract Consumption in Procurement –
- Embedded Transportation Management
- Demand Driven Manufacturing
- Manufacturing Extension for Complex Assembly Industries
- Advance Variant Configuration

Ref: SAP S/4HANA 1709 Release Highlights - SAP - Run Simple

SAP S/4HANA 1709
Key Innovations

Embedded Transportation Management
- Basic Shipping and Data Harmonization
- Integration in extended warehouse mgmt.

Consumer Products Industry
- Catch Weight Management for System Conversion

Commodity Management
- Extending pricing with the commodity pricing engine

Industry to Core
Retail / Wholesale
- Wholesale Fashion enablement; Order allocation; Segmentation

Service Core (CRM Add-On)*
- Migrate installed base CRM with eliminated middleware, harmonized data models

Manufacturing
- Demand Driven Manufacturing
- Advance Variant Configuration

Finance
- Machine Learning with SAP Cash Application
- Integration; Financial Planning

Procurement
- Centralized purchase requisitions through hub deployment
- Machine Learning for Contract Consumption

Enterprise Asset Management
- Report and Repair Malfunction
- Breakdown Analysis

Sales
- Electronic and digital payments with Integration with Payment Hub

Manufacturing
- Engineering Cockpit
- Extension for Complex Assembly Industries

Quality Management
- Manage usage decisions
- Analytics for quantitative results

Extended Warehouse Management
- advanced Labor Management
- Pallet Planning

PLM
- Visual Enterprise Generator Conversion
- Recipe Management and Recipe finder

Maximize SAP Fiori Experience
- SAP Fiori Overview Pages

Ref: SAP S/4HANA 1709 Release Highlights - SAP - Run Simple

SAP S/4HANA 1709
User Experience Enhancements

SAP Fiori 2.0
- UX evolution
- New Fiori apps

Additional SAP Fiori Overview Pages:
- sales management
- project profitability
- inventory management
- treasury management

Value Proposition
- Immediate, domain-specific insights on the tasks that need your attention
- Ability to take quick actions to solve issues.
- Easy forward navigation to related applications.

Capabilities
- Very flexible selection criteria available.
- Drill down on detail KPIs.
- Easy-to-use formats with charts, lists, and tables on a single page.

Ref: SAP S/4HANA 1709 Release Highlights - SAP - Run Simple

SAP S/4HANA 1709
New release including new technology stack

Active consumption of new SAP HANA 2 features with SAP S/4HANA 1709

- Active/Active
  = offload analytical workload to SAP HANA System Replication (secondary)
- SAP S/4HANA scale-out
  = Run largest S/4HANA systems with application-optimized data distribution

Focus on Innovation   Foster Innovation   Drive Innovation   Power Innovation

Database Management   Data   Analytical   Application
Transformed   Management   Intelligence   Development Transformed
        Transformed   Transformed

Ref: SAP S/4HANA 1709 Release Highlights - SAP - Run Simple

SAP S/4HANA for Manufacturing planning and scheduling
Comprehensive Plan to Produce in ONE System

- **PP/DS planning and scheduling features available in SAP S/4HANA**
    - Constraint-based capacity planning, scheduling & optimization
    - Heuristic framework
    - Industry-specific features (RPM, MMP & CBP)
    - Simulation versions and transactional simulation

- **Simplicity and Seamless Integration**
    - One coherent application, consistent look at feel, intuitive navigation PP/DS is an integral part of S4/HANA (not an add-on, not a side-by-side installation)
    - Simplified master data and integration model maintenance

- **Utilize HANA** (HANA only)
    - Fast MRP [One MRP for infinite planning]
    - liveCache is integral part of HANA, just one database to manage

Ref: SAP S/4HANA 1709 Release Highlights - SAP - Run Simple

Advanced Production Planning

- Multi-level production planning
- Order Pegging
- Heuristics framework:
    - Use delivered advanced planning heuristics (40+)
    - Develop own heuristics
    - Industry specific:
        - Automotive (RPM, MMP)
        - Mill (CDP)
        - Process (Res.networks, tanks, campaigns...)
- Supports various manufacturing models:
    - Make to Stock
    - Make to Order
    - Engineer to Order

Ref: SAP S/4HANA 1709 Release Highlights - SAP - Run Simple

Detailed Scheduling & Optimization

- Forward & Backward (multi-level) Constrained Scheduling
  - Constrained scheduling
  - Scheduling modes
  - Optimal sequencing
- Scheduling Optimizer
- Flexible graphical prod.operations scheduling
- Backlog Resolution
- What-if Analysis & Simulation
- Configurable exception Alert Monitor

Ref: SAP S/4HANA 1709 Release Highlights - SAP - Run Simple

HANA - The Simplifier of Enterprise Software – New Era in SAP

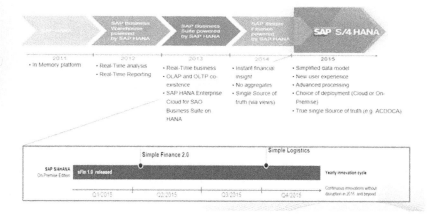

S/4 HANA – The Next generation ERP Platform – New Era in SAP

The Case for SAP S/4HANA Finance

KPI#1 - Drive integration of information across the enterprise

SAP S/4HANA Finance Key Functional Benefits: [Finance Efficiency (FE) + Business Insight (BI)]	SAP S/4HANA Finance Benchmark
• **Central Journal:** One central finance platform for the entire group with full line item detail • **One common view** of financial and operational data, to help ensure enterprise-wide consistency and reduce reconciliation time and errors. Built-in harmonization between financial and managerial accounting • **Real-time data** across all financial dimensions • **Cash and Liquidity Management:** Provide real-time insight into global sources/uses of cash • **Dept. and Investment Management:** Analyze financial exposure and advanced risk-measurement methods • **Financial Risk Management:** Assess alternative risks and scenarios to determine optimal course of action • **Commodity Risk Management:** Provide end to end visibility into commodity price positions • **Enterprise Risk Management:** Gain a better understanding of risks and link them to business value • **Controls and Compliance Management:** Enable effective reporting on policies and controls • **Access Governance:** Automate detection and prevention of access risk violations • **International Trade Management:** Streamline cross border supply chain and compliance activities • **Fraud Management:** Detect of patterns that indicate fraud, to reduce financial losses • **Audit Management:** Standardize audit planning, documentation, test procedures and reporting • **Better corporate alignment** and agility due to direct end user access to insight • Lower operational risks from fraud and other noncompliance activities	• 56 % lower treasury and cash management FTEs • 26 % increase in time spent on analyzing trend and data • 22 % lower audit cost • 39 % lower compliance & risk management FTEs • 50 % reduction in the average time required for loss documentation

KPI#2 - Drive enterprise cost reductions

SAP S/4HANA Finance Key Functional Benefits: [Finance Efficiency (FE)]	SAP S/4HANA Finance Benchmark
• **Profitability and Cost Management:** Optimize profits by better managing organizational costs • **Lease Administration (by Nakisa):** Identify and manages lease portfolio, compliant and transparent reporting, process automation and integration • **Financial Closing Cockpit:** Orchestrate all activities around the local financial close • **Receivables Management:** Holistically get insights in the credit worthiness of customers, manage receivables and collections, understand and analyze your working capital, extend the receivables function to your sales force • **Cash and Liquidity Management:** Provide real-time insight into global sources/uses of cash • **Lower IT complexity** • **Lower cost for manual report generation and data reconciliation**	• 76 % Higher Operating Margin • 61 % Reduced Finance Spending on Strategic Management • 100 % Reduction in overtime • Finance costs as a percentage of revenue various from best 0.4% to worst 1.2 % • 10% DSO reduction • 3% cash optimization • 22% reduction of closing efforts

KPI#3 - Measure / monitor business performance

SAP S/4HANA Finance Key Functional Benefits: [Business Insight (BI)]	SAP S/4HANA Finance Benchmark
• **Discover, analyze, and report:** Support financial analysis and operational decision making through consistent business insights and prediction capabilities across all Finance value map elements • **Lumira:** Discovery and visualization tool to easily understand your data and get the appropriate information out and create appropriate story boards to re-use these on a recurring basis and share the result with others • **BI Suite:** Crystal Reports and Web Intelligence, Design Studio, Analysis for Office • **InfiniteInsight:** Access to data mining and forecasting algorithms to be used by business users and not only by data scientists any more • Real-time analysis directly from operational data • On-the-fly analysis without system limitations from pre-built aggregates	• Number of days sales outstanding vary from best 43 days to worst 74 days • 420 hours less processing time at quarter end close

KPI#4 - Optimize Planning, Budgeting and Forecasting

SAP S/4HANA Finance Key Functional Benefits: [Finance Efficiency (FE) + Business Insight (BI)]	SAP S/4HANA Finance Benchmark
• **Integrated Business Planning:** Concept to integrate SAP Business Planning and Consolidation with SAP ERP to use the planning environment of BPC to do the detailed planning of ERP objects e.g. Cost Centers, Profit Centers, ... • **Cloud for Planning:** Public cloud planning solution which does not necessarily need any other SAP solution but deeply integrates with BPC to address satellite organizational units usually stuck in Excel hell • **Planning, Budgeting and Forecasting:** Streamline processes for enterprise planning, budgeting and forecasting with BPC for Netweaver running on SAP HANA	• 5% better productivity • 6% better profitability

KPI#5 - Execute Continuous Finance process improvements

SAP S/4HANA Finance Key Functional Benefits [Finance Efficiency (FE)]	SAP S/4HANA Finance Benchmark
• **Accounting and Financial Close** • **Accounting:** Support multiple international accounting standards • **Entity Close:** Streamline and automate the legal entity close • **Corporate Close:** Streamline the final consolidation process and shorten reporting cycles • **Reporting and Disclosure:** Automate publishing of reports and financial statements • **Financial Close Governance:** Establish consistent master data across subsidiaries • **Payments and Bank Communication:** Streamline communications with banks and automate payment workflows • **Receivables Management:** Automate and integrate receivables and collections • **Collaborative Invoice to Pay:** Streamline and automate invoice management processes • **Travel Management:** Control travel costs, compliance with making travel easier for employees • **Financial Shared Services:** Enable finance teams to turn administrative tasks into business services • **Real Estate Management:** Manage your property for greater profitability and compliance • **More effective management of working capital and financial risks** • **Collaborative Finance Operations**	• 61 % Lower G/L and closing costs • 26 % Fewer days to close annual books • 25 % faster month-end consolidation cycle • Working days to close annual books vary from best 7 days to worst 22 days • 44 % Fewer FTEs in transactional processes • 37 % lower overdue accounts receivable

KPI#6 - Provide inputs to enterprise strategy

SAP S/4HANA Finance Key Functional Benefits: [Business Insight (BI)]	SAP S/4HANA Finance Benchmark
• **Strategy Management:** Translate strategy throughout the organization with a scorecard approach by using strategy development and translation solutions from SAP. Capture cross-functional, qualitative, and quantitative performance measures and determine the interrelationship of each task to one another. Cascade scorecards, metrics, and targets to clarify priorities, drive accountability, and improve collaboration. • Extended simulation flexibility and speed through on-the-fly calculation capabilities • Built-in ability to use prediction, simulation, and analysis to evaluate the financial implications of strategic business options • Better business advice due to more relevant and timely insight	

KPI#7 - Develop talent in the finance organization

SAP S/4HANA Finance Key Functional Benefits: [Business Insight (BI)]	SAP S/4HANA Finance Benchmark
• **Fiori:** Modern user experience, independent from the respective device, HTML5 based • Improved automation capabilities to get rid of transactional activities – free-up resources for value add tasks	• Less end user training as all applications have the same look and feel • Less transactional activities, more time for creative work

1.2 HANA Goals

- ✓ Enables New Application and Optimize Existing Application
- ✓ High Performance and Scalability
- ✓ Hybrid Data Management System
- ✓ Compatible with Standard DBMS feature
- ✓ Support for Text analysis, indexing and search
- ✓ Cloud support and application isolation
- ✓ Executing application logic inside the data layer

SAP HANA Vendors

SAP has partnered with leading IT hardware vendors, like IBM, Dell, Cisco etc. and combined it with SAP licensed services and technology to sell SAP HANA platform.

There are, total, 11 vendors which manufacture HANA Appliances & provide onsite support for installation and configuration of HANA system.

Top few Vendors include:

- ✓ IBM
- ✓ Dell
- ✓ HP
- ✓ Cisco
- ✓ Fujitsu
- ✓ Lenovo (China)
- ✓ NEC
- ✓ Huawei

According to statistics provided by SAP, IBM is one of major vendor of SAP HANA hardware appliances and has a market share of 50-52% but according to another market survey conducted by HANA clients, **IBM has a market hold up to 70%**.

SAP HANA Installation

HANA Hardware vendors provide preconfigured appliances for hardware, Operating System & SAP software product.

Vendor finalizes the installation by an onsite setup & configuration of HANA components. This onsite visit includes deployment of HANA system in Data Center, connectivity to Organization Network, SAP system ID adaption, updates from Solution Manager, SAP Router Connectivity, SSL enablement and other system configuration.

Customer/Client starts with connectivity of Data Source system and BI clients. HANA Studio Installation is completed on local system & HANA system is added to perform Data modeling and administration.

SAP HANA – IN-MEMORY-COMPUTING ENGINE

An In-Memory database means all the data from source system is stored in a RAM memory. In a conventional Database system, all data is stored in hard disk. SAP HANA In-Memory Database wastes no time in loading the data from hard disk to RAM. It provides faster access of data to multicore CPUs for information processing and analysis.

Features of In-Memory Database

The main features of SAP HANA in-memory database are:

- SAP HANA is Hybrid In-memory database.

- It combines row based, column based and Object Oriented base technology.

- It uses parallel processing with multicore CPU Architecture.

- Conventional Database reads memory data in 5 milliseconds. SAP HANA In-Memory database reads data in 5 nanoseconds.

It means, memory reads in HANA database are 1 million times faster than a conventional database hard disk memory reads.

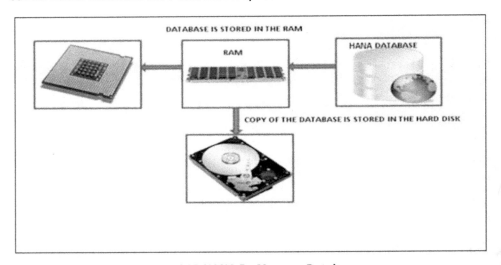

SAP HANA In-Memory Database

Ref: Tutorialspoint

Analysts want to see current data immediately in real time and do not want to wait for data until it is loaded to SAP BW system. SAP HANA In-Memory processing allows loading of real time data with the use of various data provisioning techniques.

Advantages of In-Memory Database

- HANA database takes advantage of in-memory processing to deliver the fastest data-retrieval speeds, which is enticing to companies struggling with high-scale online transactions or timely forecasting and planning.

- Disk-based storage is still the enterprise standard and price of RAM has been declining steadily, so memory-intensive architectures will eventually replace slow, mechanical spinning disks and will lower the cost of data storage.

- In-Memory Column-based storage provides data compression up to 11 times, thus, reducing the storage space of huge data.

- This speed advantages offered by RAM storage system are further enhanced by the use of multi-core CPUs, multiple CPUs per node and multiple nodes per server in a distributed environment.

1.3 The Power of HANA

- Give business users the power to investigate and visualize their data with advanced analytic tools.

- Power applications that deliver real-time insights to drive more effective and timely decision making.

- Accelerate analytics, business processes, data processing, and predictive capabilities to run business in real-time.

- Quickly setup, deploy, and build real-time applications that feature mobile, collaboration, big data, and analytics services.

Capabilities	Customer Value
Columnar data storage	Data Compression
In-memory storage	Faster Aggregation
In-memory computation	Faster Calculation time
Integration with live replication	Real time analytics
No pre-aggregated tables	Simpler BI modelling
Direct usage of predictive functionality	Plug & Play

1.4 Introduction of HANA – HANA Directions

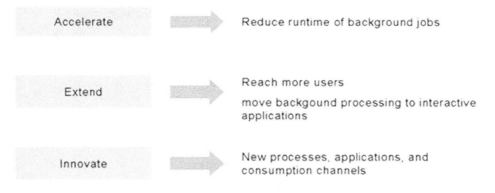

1.5 Overall HANA Architecture

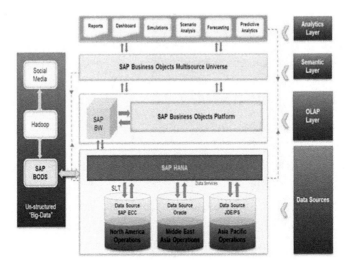

SAP HANA was initially, developed in Java and C++ and designed to run only on Operating System Suse Linux Enterprise Server 11. SAP HANA system consists of multiple components that are responsible to emphasize computing power of HANA system.

- Most important component of SAP HANA system is Index Server, which contains SQL/MDX processor to handle query statements for database.

- HANA system contains Name Server, Preprocessor Server, Statistics Server and XS engine, which is used to communicate and host small web applications and various other components.

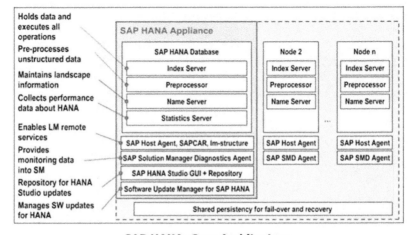

SAP HANA: Core Architecture

Ref: tutorialspoint

Index Server

Index Server is heart of SAP HANA database system. It contains actual data and engines for processing that data. When SQL or MDX is fired for SAP HANA system, an Index Server takes care of all these requests and processes them. All HANA processing takes place in Index Server.

Index Server contains Data engines to handle all SQL/MDX statements that come to HANA database system. It also has Persistence Layer that is responsible for durability of HANA system and ensures HANA system is restored to most recent state when there is restart of system failure.

Index Server also has Session and Transaction Manager, which manage transactions and keep track of all running and closed transactions.

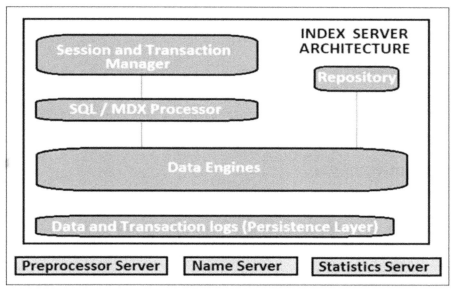

Ref: tutorialspoint

Index Server: Architecture

SQL/MDX Processor

It is responsible for processing SQL/MDX transactions with data engines responsible to run queries. It segments all query requests and direct them to correct engine for the performance Optimization.

It also ensures that all SQL/MDX requests are authorized and also provide error handling for efficient processing of these statements. It contains several engines and processors for query execution:

✓ MDX (Multi Dimension Expression) is query language for OLAP systems like SQL is used for Relational database. MDX Engine is responsible to handle queries and manipulates multidimensional data stored in OLAP cubes.

✓ Planning Engine is responsible to run planning operations within SAP HANA database.

✓ Calculation Engine converts data into Calculation models to create logical execution plan to support parallel processing of statements.

✓ Stored Procedure processor executes procedure calls for optimized processing; it converts OLAP cubes to HANA optimized cubes.

Transaction and Session Management

It is responsible to coordinate all database transactions and keep track of all running and closed transactions.

When a transaction is executed or failed, Transaction manager notifies relevant data engine to take necessary actions.

Session management component is responsible to initialize and manage sessions and connections for SAP HANA system using predefined session parameters.

Persistence Layer

It is responsible for durability and atomicity of transactions in HANA system. Persistence layer provides built in disaster recovery system for HANA database.

It ensures database is restored to most recent state and ensures that all the transactions are completed or undone in case of a system failure or restart.

It is also responsible to manage data and transaction logs and also contain data backup, log backup and configuration back of HANA system. Backups are stored as save points in the Data Volumes via a Save Point coordinator, which is normally set to take back every 5-10 minutes.

Preprocessor Server

Preprocessor Server in SAP HANA system is used for text data analysis.

Index Server uses preprocessor server for analyzing text data and extracting the information from text data when text search capabilities are used.

Name Server

NAME server contains System Landscape information of HANA system. In distributed environment, there are multiple nodes with each node having multiple CPU's, Name server holds topology of HANA system and has information about all the running components and information is spread on all the components.

- Topology of SAP HANA system is recorded here.
- It decreases the time in re-indexing as it holds which data is on which server in distributed environment.

Statistical Server

This server checks and analyzes the health of all components in HANA system. Statistical Server is responsible for collecting the data related to system resources, their allocation and consumption of the resources and overall performance of HANA system.

It also provides historical data related to system performance for analyses purpose, to check and fix performance related issues in HANA system.

XS Engine

XS engine helps external Java and HTML based applications to access HANA system with the help of XS client. As SAP HANA system contains a web server which can be used to host small JAVA/HTML based applications.

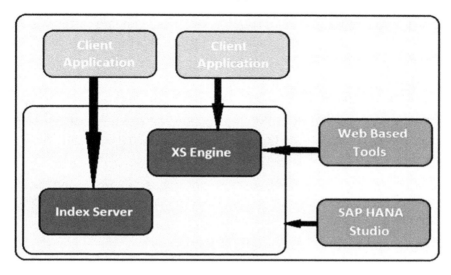

SAP HANA: XS Engine
Ref: tutorialspoint

XS Engine transforms the persistence model stored in database into consumption model for clients exposed via HTTP/HTTPS.

SAP Host Agent

SAP Host agent should be installed on all the machines that are part of SAP HANA system Landscape. SAP Host agent is used by Software Update Manager SUM for installing automatic updates to all components of HANA system in distributed environment.

LM Structure

LM structure of SAP HANA system contains information about current installation details. This information is used by Software Update Manager to install automatic updates on HANA system components.

SAP Solution Manager (SAP SOLMAN) diagnostic Agent

This diagnostic agent provides all data to SAP Solution Manager to monitor SAP HANA system. This agent provides all the information about HANA database, which include database current state and general information.

It provides configuration details of HANA system when SAP SOLMAN is integrated with SAP HANA system.

SAP HANA Studio Repository

SAP HANA studio repository helps HANA developers to update current version of HANA studio to latest versions. Studio Repository holds the code which does this update.

Software Update Manager for SAP HANA

SAP Market Place is used to install updates for SAP systems. Software Update Manager for HANA system helps in update of HANA system from SAP Market place.

It is used for software downloads, customer messages, SAP Notes and requesting license keys for HANA system. It is also used to distribute HANA studio to end user's systems.

1.6 SAP Business Suite Powered by SAP HANA

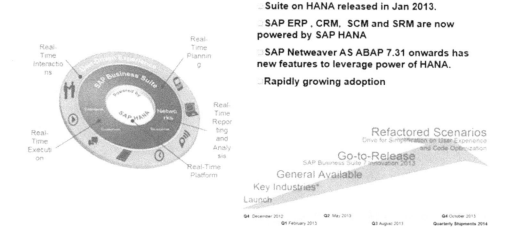

The Most Modern Business Platform for Innovation Without Disruption

- Suite on HANA released in Jan 2013.
- SAP ERP , CRM, SCM and SRM are now powered by SAP HANA
- SAP Netweaver AS ABAP 7.31 onwards has new features to leverage power of HANA.
- Rapidly growing adoption

1.7 Introduction of HANA – HANA Studio

SAP HANA studio is an Eclipse-based tool. SAP HANA studio is both, the central development environment and the main administration tool for HANA system. Additional features are:

- It is a client tool, which can be used to access local or remote HANA system,

- It provides an environment for HANA Administration, HANA Information Modeling and Data Provisioning in HANA database.

SAP HANA Studio can be used on following platforms:

- Microsoft Windows 32 and 64 bit versions of: Windows XP, Windows Vista, Windows 7.

- SUSE Linux Enterprise Server SLES11: x86 64 bit.

- Mac OS, HANA studio client is not available.

Depending on HANA Studio installation, not all features may be available. At the time of Studio installation, specify the features you want to install as per the role. To work on most recent version of HANA studio, Software Life Cycle Manager can be used for client update.

Central Facts

Eclipse-Based

- Widely-accepted development environment
- Tools based on existing Eclipse frameworks
- Common development environment for SAP HANA and ABAP (ADT) going forward

Several Perspectives

- A perspective is a window within the Eclipse workbench that provides functions related to a particular task:
  - Administration
  - Modeling

Views

- Each perspective is made up of a number of panes called views
  - Navigator
  - Table Editor...

Perspectives

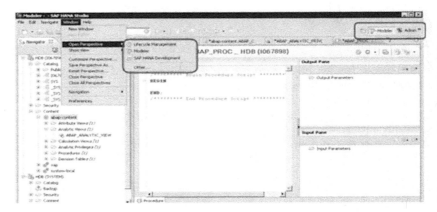

The Modeler Perspective

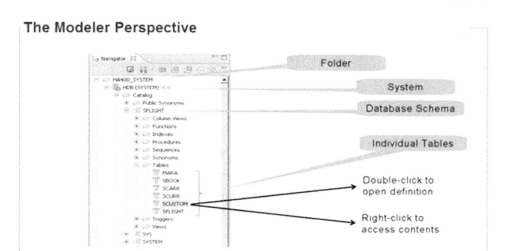

System

To connect to a system you need

- Hostname
- Instance Number
- Description
- User
- Password
- (Port is automatically generated)

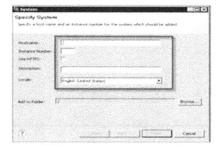

Creating Content Package

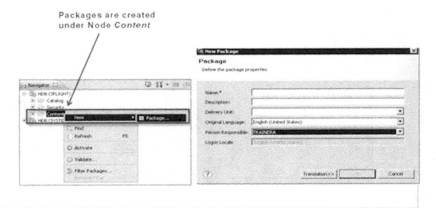

Packages are created
under Node *Content*

CHAPTER 2

General Programming Standards

2.1 Naming Conventions

- ✓ All custom ABAP/4 program names will follow the naming standards stated in the *ABAP/4 Naming Standards* artefact.

- ✓ Each ABAP/4 program should abide by the ABAP internal naming conventions set forth in this artefact.

2.2 ABAP/4 Performance

All programs should be written to maximize performance. Throughout this artefact there are suggestions as to which approaches are most efficient. Additional documents that address ABAP/4 performance are available from the technical lead.

2.2.1 Take ABAP to HANA – Performance Rules and Guidelines

Keep the result sets small	Don't retrieve rows from the database and discard them on the application server using CHECK or EXIT, e.g. in SELECT loops
	Make the WHERE clause as specific as possible
Minimize amount of transferred data	Use SELECT with a field list instead of SELECT * in order to transfer just the columns you really need
	Use aggregate functions (COUNT, MIN, MAX, SUM, AVG) instead of transferring all the rows to the application server
Minimize the number of data transfers	Use JOINs and / or sub-queries instead of nested SELECT loops
	Use SELECT ... FOR ALL ENTRIES instead of lots of SELECTs or SELECT SINGLEs
	Use array variants of INSERT, UPDATE, MODIFY, and DELETE
Minimize the search overhead	Define and use appropriate secondary indexes
Keep load away from the database	Avoid reading data redundancy
	Use table buffering (if applicable) and do not bypass it
	Sort data in your ABAP programs

- **Classical Approach (Non HANA): Minimize the number of data transfers**
- **New Approach (in ABAP on HANA): No Change**
- **Additions in the context of SAP HANA**

As on all database systems, there is a small performance overhead associated with every request for connection handling, SQL parsing, execution plan determination, etc..

Avoiding such frequent single database requests is more important on SAP HANA.

In particular, the following existing guidelines should be prioritized higher on SAP HANA:

- For modifying operations (INSERT, UPDATE, DELETE) using array operations should be preferred to single operations when changing many data records.
- Nested SELECT loops should be avoided or replaced if possible by Changing the nested single SELECT statement to an appropriate SQL construct (e.g. FOR ALL ENTRIES, JOIN, sub-query, etc.) .
- Using the ABAP table buffer.

Important: In addition, reducing the selected field list to the actually needed columns should be prioritized higher on SAP HANA in case of statements which are either executed very frequently, or which return large result sets.

- **Classical Approach: Minimize the search overhead**
- **New Approach (in ABAP on HANA): No Change**
- **Additions in the context of SAP HANA**

  In most cases SAP HANA does not require secondary indices for good search performance. To reduce main memory consumption and to improve insert performance all existing non-unique secondary database indices on columnar tables are removed during migration or do not get created during installation for all AS ABAP systems from SAP NetWeaver 7.4 onwards.

  For some use cases secondary indexes can still be beneficial. This is especially true for highly selective queries on non-primary key fields. These queries can be significantly improved by indexes on single fields which are most selective.

- **Classical Approach (Non HANA): Keep load away from the database**
- **New Approach (in ABAP on HANA): Push data-intensive calculations to the database where applicable**

- **Additions in the context of SAP HANA**

  On SAP HANA, it is beneficial to move data-intensive calculations into the database. Nevertheless, it is not recommended to execute the same operations redundantly, e.g. in different user contexts or different dialog steps of the same user. Meaningful buffering of results on the application server should be applied.

The following existing recommendations should be considered in this light on SAP HANA

- **Sorting data:** In general, the recommendations for sorting remain as before, i.e. if the database does not use the same index for sorting as for selection, then it may be more efficient to sort data in the application server. However, if on SAP HANA the sorting is part of a larger calculation logic (e.g. within a procedure), it should be done in SAP HANA.

- **Using logical databases:** The general guidelines regarding logical databases remain the same. However, using logical databases does not provide performance advantages compared to a proper usage of Open SQL.

Performance Guidelines Scenarios	Non-Hana DB	HANA DB
Database select inside Loop	Replace with Select..For All Entries or Inner Join	Replace with Select..For All Entries or Inner Join or Appropriate SQL Script
Insert/Update/Delete Inside Loop	Replace with Array Operation	Replace with Array Operation
Use of Check statement inside Select..EndSelect	Should be avoided	Should be avoided
Use of Select..EndSelect / Nested Selects	Replace with Select..For All Entries or Inner Join. In some scenario we may need to use Select..EndSelect while fetching huge number of records by packets to avoid time out.	Replace with Select..For All Entries or Inner Join or Appropriate SQL Script. HANA Views. Time out will not occur to fetch huge number of records
Use of Select *	Fetch the fields which are required. Generally if 60% of the fields are used we can do a Select *	Fetch the fields which are required. Impact is more in HANA so never use Select * even if 90% fields are used
Use aggregate functions (COUNT, MIN, MAX, SUM, AVG)	Use this instead of fetching all the records	Use this instead of fetching all the records
Use of Where Clause with No available index	Performance can be Impacted if it's a huge table	Performance will not be impacted compared to other DB
Use of Table buffering	Use Table buffer without bypassing it	Use Table buffer without bypassing it
Sort data in Database	Sorting is done in application server after data selection	Sorting should be done in the database by Order By clause
Use of Index Table	Use is Mandatory for performance improvement	Can be replaced by Open SQL or SQL script but optional
Use of Cluster Tables	Sorting is default – no explicit sort is required	Order By Clause is required to add in the select
Perform unit/date conversions in Database	Do it in application server	Do it in Database

2.2.2   Take ABAP to HANA – Optimize Conventional Code using Tools

Classic Runtime Analysis (SE30) & ABAP Trace (SAT)

- The functions of the classic Runtime Analysis (SE30) and the new ABAP Trace (SAT) can be completely used in the HANA Context
- The new ABAP Trace replaces the classical Runtime Analysis
- Both tools measure runtime of processing blocks (methods, functions, subroutines) or single statements
- No database-specific functions are available

ABAP Trace (SAT)

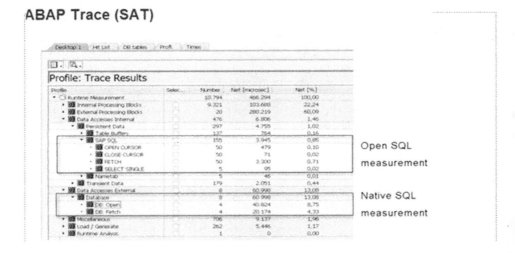

Code Inspector

The existing rules and guidelines checked by Code Inspector are still valid in the context of HANA

For NW 7.40 the following additional HANA checks are planned:

- SELECTS in LOOPs across modularization units
- Problematic SELECT * statements (where less than a certain percentage of the fields are subsequently used)
- Find SELECT...FOR ALL ENTRIES statements that can be replaced by a join

SQL Trace (ST05)

Use SQL Trace (ST05) to

- Display record of all database access
  (including SQL calls over a secondary database connection)
- Detect redundant / identical SELECT statements
- Locate database-related performance issues
- Display database execution plan for statements
  (SAP HANA execution plans planned for NW 7.40)

2.3   Program Attributes

Program attributes are set from the "Attributes" option on the initial ABAP/4 editor screen as applicable. All program attributes for an ABAP are to be set as follows as applicable. :

2.3.1   Title

The title should be a short concise description as applicable.   This is the title which appears in the header section of a report when it is executed.

Example:

Create BDC Session for Transaction MM01 - Create Material Master

2.3.2   Type

'1' for on-line programs which will be run on-line or in background.

'I'   for ABAP programs which cannot be run on their own but are included in another report using INCLUDE.

'M' for the module pool processing the flow logic of a screen painter dynpro or ABAP/4 transaction.

'V' for direct data base update tasks.

'F' for function pools.

'S'   for external subroutine programs.

2.3.3   Status

'P' SAP standard production program.

'K' Custom-developed program for production.

'T' Program that will never be in production.

2.3.4   Application

'Z' Customer branch

2.3.5 Authorization Group

This is used to restrict access to users with a matching authorization group in their profile. Checks are performed before report execution, and before access to utility functions, report attributes, and the ABAP/4 editor as applicable.

2.3.6 Logical Database

Assigns the logical database to be evaluated by the program. The workbench provides access to all logical database programs delivered by SAP as applicable.

2.3.7 From Application

Used in conjunction with the logical database field. The tables retrieved to access the particular logical database depend upon this entry as applicable.

2.3.8 Screen

This is for report programs only. If a Screen is not specified the system will create a selection screen based on the logical database (if specified), the program parameters and select-options. To use an existing selection screen, enter the version in this field. Versions are connected to the programming of logical databases. Use the workbench to analyze logical database screen versions as applicable.

2.3.9 Upper/Lower Case

To display the program code in lowercase while in the ABAP/4 Editor, this field is left blank. If marked, program code is in uppercase as applicable.

2.3.10 Editor Lock

To be set while a program is being created or modified. It allows only the user who set the flag to modify the program. This is to prevent alteration of a program while a programmer makes modifications to it as applicable.

As a standard, use the Workbench Organizer as a locking mechanism when changing objects. This will reduce the number of changes when a program is ready to be transported to the test or production environment as applicable.

2.3.11 Fixed Point Arithmetic

If flagged, all calculations in the program are done using fixed point arithmetic. All programs that contain calculations should have this flag set. If the field is not set, decimal places are only taken into consideration for output, not for calculations as applicable.

2.3.12 Start via Variant

If set, the program can only be executed via variant as applicable.

2.4 Comments, Formatting, Structure

2.4.1 Comments

Internal commenting of an ABAP/4 is essential for program maintenance and must be done for all ABAP/4 programs as applicable.

- It is advisable to provide future programmers with documentation of purpose, changes, enhancements, additions, and deletions. Explain the purpose, design, structure and any testing hints at the top of the program. Maintain a chronological history of modification notes; with the latest change being the last entry in the modification log. The documentation block will be placed at the top of the main program. An overall description of the program will be given at the top of the program and will have the following format:

Example:

```
***********************************************************************
* Report  <insert report name here>
*---------------------------------------------------------------*
*------------ This line contains the program title  --------------*
*
* Description  : <Program Description>
*
* Specification : <Specification Name>
* Change #     : <For support related activities>
*
*
* Input      : <Input>
* Output     : <Output>
*
* Creation date : <Date in format DD-MMM-YYYY>
* Author     : <Authorn Name>
*---------------------------------------------------------------*
* Number   : 1              Author   :
* Date     : DD/MM/YYYY          Type    : Change
* Code     : <your initials>0001     OBJECT ID #  :
* Change # :
*
* Description :  Add new field in....

                 *---------------------------------------------------------------*
```

If you are creating an Include, Function Module, etc. then you must still place the above header block at the top of the program using the pattern button.

- All documentation will be maintained using the documentation feature through the menu toolbar Goto -> Program Doc. Enter in the following details in the body of the banner:
    - ✓ Description : Lists and describes processing steps done in the program.
    - ✓ Precondition: Lists any input and processing that is necessary before executing the program.
    - ✓ Output: Lists any output from the program.
    - ✓ SAP Function: List of SAP functions used by the program.
    - ✓ Transactions Called: List of SAP transactions called in the program.
    - ✓ Programs Called: Lists all programs called by the ABAP program.
    - ✓ Example: Illustrates an example of the program code.

- If a modification is made to an existing ABAP/4 program, an entry must be made in the "CHANGES" section with the date, programmer's name, change request number, and a brief description.

- If an ABAP/4 program is being changed to apply an OSS note, it is essential that the OSS note number appear as a comment at the end of each line of code added. If the OSS note requires deletion of code, the code must be commented out (not deleted) and the OSS note number must appear at the end of the deleted line. If a large block of code is being maintained, it is acceptable to mark the beginning and the end of the change with a comment that includes the OSS note number. ABAP/4 code will be written modular rather than in line paragraph or form style.

2.4.2   Formatting

2.4.2.1 FORMS

A large and complex string of coding statements must be broken up and placed in FORMs to provide easy readability and maintainability as applicable.

- FORMs are subroutines which allow a programmer to define a process once in a program and call that routine from different places within the program. If a block of code is executed more than once, it shall be placed in a subroutine. When creating the FORM with Workbench, it will be created in an Include and placed at the bottom of the code. This makes the code more readable, requires less indentation, and is easier to debug since the debugger can jump through an entire subroutine via a PF key.

- Each FORM should serve only one function and should not be more than one printed page long.

- FORMs will be placed at the end of the ABAP in the Include - defaulted by Workbench. The function of the form will be described in the comment section. In the case of FORMs that use parameters, the parameters will also be described.

- FORM names must begin with F_. This will display all the program objects together when using Workbench. The rest of the FORM name will describe what the FORM is doing.

- Use the SAP default FORM comment box. To use this feature, code the PERFORM statement and then double click on the new form name. The FORM and ENDFORM statements and a default comment box will be generated at the end of the ABAP. If any parameters are passed in the PERFORM, comment lines allowing individual description of these parameters will be generated as well.

- The format parameters must be typed using TYPE keywords. This is a performance feature and also allows one to correct typing errors before runtime.

- Pass input parameters as using parameters and output parameters as CHANGING parameters. If in doubt, pass the parameters by value.

- To avoid shadowing problems, always name your formal parameters different to the actual parameters.

Example:

- Includes will be used to break down large programs into sections that can be maintained more easily and to create program sections that can be shared by several programs. INCLUDE statements will be commented individually by using the comment indication '*'. Code contained within the INCLUDE statement must adhere to programming standards and naming conventions as applicable.

Example:

```
* Insert a descriptive text to describe the INCLUDE * INCLUDE  xxxxxxxx.
```

- For overall legibility, an ABAP/4 Report will be neatly indented. The PRETTY PRINTER command (PP typed in the command line) can be used to indent each nested command structure by 2 positions. This is an easy command which should be run at the end of coding to make the structure uniform.

- Statements with multiple objects must be indented and aligned for clarity.

2.4.2.2 Text Elements

Each ABAP should have associated text elements and constants from the source code placed within the Text Elements section of the ABAP/4 Editor as applicable.

Titles and Headings - The heading will always be completed in as much detail as possible. Use of standard headings is preferred as they can be easily made multilingual. The alternative is coded headings which will require further coding for each language supported. Note: Any data entered here will not show up in the report header if the program uses the "No Standard Page Heading" phrase and codes a custom header.

Selection Texts - All system SELECT-OPTIONS and PARAMETERS are limited to 8 characters and as a consequence must always have selection texts set to improve user understanding.

Text-Symbols - As a standard, use the following example.

Example:

```
WRITE: / TEXT-001.
```

The advantage of this method is ease of maintainability if TEXT-001 is coded several times in the program and needs to be changed. The editor command REPLACE does not change contents inside single quotes.

Use the text symbol in the format TEXT-XXX, do not use the format 'Free Text'(XXX).

2.4.2.3 Formatting Commands

Example:

Correct

WRITE: / 01   xxxxxxx1,
      10   xxxxxxx2,
      15   xxxxxxx3.

Incorrect
WRITE: / 01   xxxxxxx1, 10   xxxxxxx2, 15   xxxxxxx3.

- Use one line per object when defining multiple objects of the same entity. Describe those objects on that same line.

Example:

Correct
IF V_X = 3   **AND V_Y = 2**   **AND V_Z = 1.**   **PERFORM….**   **ENDIF.**
Incorrect
IF V_X = 3 AND V_Y =2 AND V_Z = 1   **PERFORM….**   **ENDIF.**

2.4.3   ABAP/4 Coding Structure

The standard structure for ABAP/4 Report coding is shown below with header created as per pattern described above.

It is always recommended to modularize the program into unitz viz., includes – one for selection screen, one for data declaration, one for subroutines….

REPORT ….

```
* * * * * * * * * * * * * * * * * * * * * * * * * * * * * * * * * * * * * * * * * * * * * * * * * * * * *
*
* Data Declarations Section
*
***************************************************
TYPES OR TYPE-POOLS
PARAMETERS
```

```
SELECT-OPTIONS
TABLES
DATA
FIELD-GROUPS
FIELDS
FIELD-SYMBOLS


* * * * * * * * * * * * * * * * * * * * * * * * * * * * * * * * * * * * * * * * * * * * * * * * * *
*
* Events Section
*
****************************************************
INITIALIZATION                                          AT SELECTION-SCREEN
                          START-OF-SELECTION
             GET
END-OF-SELECTION                                          TOP-OF-PAGE
                          END-OF-PAGE
* * * * * * * * * * * * * * * * * * * * * * * * * * * * * * * * * * * * * * * * * * * * * * * * *
*
* Control Section
*
****************************************************
TOP-OF-PAGE DURING LINE-SELECTION
AT LINE-SELECTION
AT PFnn
AT USER-COMMAND


* * * * * * * * * * * * * * * * * * * * * * * * * * * * * * * * * * * * * * * * * * * * * * * * * *
*
* Subroutines
*
****************************************************
* Any optional elements (E.g. FORMS) are in this section
```

2.4.4 Modular Program Structure

Module programs should only contain Include statements and any necessary comments.

2.4.4.1 Screen Flow Logic

Place the AT EXIT COMMAND at the beginning of the flow logic.

Example:

PROCESS AFTER INPUT.	MODULE
EXIT_1170 AT EXIT-COMMAND.	MODULE PAI_1170.

Use FIELD and CHAIN statements to keep fields in error open for correction.

Example:

PROCESS AFTER INPUT.	
MODULE EXIT_1170 AT EXIT-COMMAND.	
CHAIN.	
FIELD BTCH1170-JOBNAME.	
FIELD BTCH1170-USERNAME.	
FIELD BTCH1170-FROM_DATE.	
FIELD BTCH1170-FROM_TIME.	
MODULE PAI_1170.	ENDCHAIN.

When using the AT CURSOR SELECTION, code it after the AT EXIT-COMMAND.

2.4.4.2 SCREENS

- When designing SCREENS, place fields on the screen in the sequence in which they are most frequently used.
- Align all labels and fields with neighbouring lines and BOX any related screen fields together.
- Position the cursor to the most frequently used field on the initial screen display.
- For screen fields that require text input, place literal labels on the left and the data entry fields on the right of the label.
- For screen fields that use graphical elements, place the literal label to the right of the graphic element.

2.4.5 GUI Status

- For each GUI, use SAP defaults proposed by Menu Painter within Workbench for Menu as applicable.
- Create a title bar for each screen within a transaction that identifies what function and area the screen is to be used for.
- The standard set of PF Keys must use the SAP defaults proposed by Menu Painter from Workbench.
- On all initial entry screens, be sure the BACK, CANCEL, and EXIT functions are activated.
- The following functions should have a standard function code associated to them:

Function	Function Code	Function Type
ADD	ADD	
CHANGE	CHNG	
DELETE	DELT	
DISPLAY	DISP	
SAVE	SAVE	
BACK	BACK	
CANCEL	CANC	E
EXIT	EXIT	E
CHOOSE	CHSE	
FIRST PAGE	P--	
PREVIOUS PAGE	P-	
NEXT PAGE	P+	
LAST PAGE	P++	
PRINT	PRNT	

2.5   Multi-Language coding

All programs should be coded so that they can be used under multiple logon languages. Hard-coding of language keys or text that will appear as output must be avoided as applicable. Text elements should be used so that the program can refer to the text element. The text elements can be translated into any languages required.

2.6   Object Oriented Programming

Recommended to create all new custom developments using object oriented programming which is future programming techniques as applicable.

2.7 SAP Smart Forms vs. SAPScript

New printed forms should be developed using SAP Smart Forms rather than SAPScript as applicable.

2.8 Core Modifications

Modifications to core R/3 programs should be avoided as applicable.

All alternatives to a core modification must be explored. These are documented in the R/3 Library→Basis Components→ABAP Workbench→Changing the SAP Standard. The alternatives include Transaction Variants, Screen Variants, Selection Variants, GuiXT, Menu Exits, Screen Exits, Function Module Exits, Open-FI and Business Add-Ins.

In ECC 6.0, enhancement framework concept (New BADI, Explicit Enhancement, and Implicit Enhancements) enables integration of different concepts of modifying and enhancing development objects which can be thoroughly analyzed and reviewed as one of the alternative options.

Accepted only for:

- OSS Notes (Automatic/Manual)
- Few user-exits (mainly related to Sales & Distribution module) which have to be implemented by modifying a standard include.
- Customizing activity requiring modification key (E.g., Pricing procedure routines, requirements etc.)

Changes should be made by using the Modification Assistant if possible.

- When making modifications to SAP core programs, it is very important to document the changes made within the program. Within the comments section at the beginning of the program, include the following as part of a modification log:
  - ◊ Change Request # of the modification (system assigned)
  - ◊ Sequence number
  - ◊ Name of the person making the modification
  - ◊ Date
  - ◊ Description of the modification

Example:

```
*************************************************Program
xxxxxxxx                    *Description: ............
                            *-------------------------------------------
* CHANGES:
*
* 1)  Date                  : mm/dd/yyyy.
*     Programmer            : _____
*     Repair #              : _____
*     Description of change :
*
*
*************************************************
```

- If a modification is made to an existing ABAP/4 program, an entry must be made in the "CHANGES" section (shown above) with the sequence number, date, programmer's name, repair number, and a brief description.

- Changes should be made by using the modification assistant or by using the following procedure: In the body of the ABAP, any line to be removed or changed must be commented out. Both the new and old line should contain the sequence number at the end of the line. E.g:

```
*        WRITE: ............                    " <1>
         WRITE: new variables                  " <1>
```

If the change affects a large number of lines then it is not necessary to place the sequence # at the end of every line (as shown above). Instead, mark the start of the block with:

```
*----- `Start <Sequence #>------
```

and mark the end of the block with:

```
*-----`End <Sequence #>--------
```

E.g:

```
*----- `Start <1> ------
SELECT ......
         .

         .

         .
     .END-SELECT.
*----- `End <1> ------
```

2.9   Screen Personas

SAP Screen Personas offers a simple drag and drop approach to modify any common SAP GUI screens to improve user friendliness, visual enhancements and help accomplish an array of tasks within minimal investment in resources.

Overview

SAP Screen Personas is a new age UI tool that is redefining the way business processes are being implemented and screens are being designed, taking into consideration the growing expectations from the SAP users. Customers are looking for simple and user-friendly SAP systems that eliminates the clutter and complexity of typical business processes that their users encounter, and at the same time providing a great look and feel for the screens that they encounter on a day to day basis. SAP Screen Personas offers intuitive screens that enhance usability – integrates functionality, performance and user experience. Simply stated, companies can simplify their screens by eliminating fields they don't use, converting free text entry to pull down menus and automating steps that they use frequently.

With more intuitive SAP screens, organizations can improve user satisfaction, improve training time and optimize resources on screen modifications. SAP Screen Personas offers one of the best methods to enhance SAP usability.

SAP Personas complements SAP Fiori

There are many similarities between SAP Screen Personas and SAP Fiori, since both are targeted towards providing an improvised user experience. The following table helps you understand how SAP Personas complements SAP Fiori.

Parameters	SAP Screen Personas	SAP Fiori
Types of tasks	Specialized routine tasks	Routine tasks
Transaction Support	All SAP GUI transactions	Most of the mundane transactions
Out of box functionality	Personalize any transaction in minutes.	Ready to run
Core focus	Desktop (Windows & Mac)	Smartphones, tablets, desktop
Personalization aspects	Allows you to modify any aspect of the SAP GUI, suiting your specific business requirements.	Eliminates modifications as SAP Fiori runs out-of-box on any device.

System Architecture

SAP Screen Personas components

SAP Screen Personas works on 4 components:

- SAP Netweaver ABAP Basis
- Kernel / ITS
- Personas add-on (installs on server)
- Personas app (runs in browser)

SAP Screen Personas components

You can install SAP Screen Personas through one of the two server modes, i.e. central server or independent servers.

Benefits

Technical Benefits

- Provides a single UX entry point for all SAP application designs :
  - Use SAP Screen Personas to enhance any Dynpro screen into the Fiori design.
  - Launch SAP Screen Personas transactions from any of the platforms: Browser, Fiori Launchpad, NWBC or SAP Portal.
- Provides an intuitive suite on SAP HANA experience :
  - Simplify any of the 10,000+ SAP GUI transaction screens for which no smart Business Cockpit, Factsheet or Fiori app exists.
- Enables seamless migration to cloud :
  - Access any SAP GUI transaction through browser.
  - Eliminate SAP GUI dependency (no need to install any client on desktop systems).

Business Benefits

- Improve employee productivity in terms of percentage of time spent on data entry.
- Simplify the user interaction through SAP – enhance adoption of business processes.
- Reduce the overall employee training costs.
- Minimize rework and ensure data quality.
- Improve your company's image and branding.
- Minimize personalization costs

Core technical requirements

- Unicode
- NetWeaver 7.40 SP3 BASIS or later
- Kernel 7.40 (gets updated to 7.42 at start of the ramp-up process)
- Skilled resources who are experts in SAP Personas to troubleshoot any issues.

SAP Personas: Scope and limitations

You can modify most classic screens in SAP using SAP Personas. Technically, you can initiate the development of the SAP Screen Personas with the standard SAP transaction screen – modify through a simple drag and drop interface. Subsequently, you can incorporate scripts, buttons, dropdown lists and other elements and at advanced level, you can use information caching and hiding to enhance the processing speed.

Coming to SAP Screen Personas limitations, it doesn't work with CRM and SRM systems, which incorporate different screen rendering technology.

CHAPTER 3

ABAP Internal Names

3.1 Data Types

- All data types used by a program must first be defined to the ABAP/4 Dictionary as a TYPE-GROUP. One or more TYPE-GROUPS can be used by the TYPE-POOLS statement as applicable.

- With the release of 3.0 there is a clear distinction between the data type and the data object:

- Data types are declared by using the keyword TYPE. Data types are pure type descriptions. They do not require any storage space. A data type characterizes the technical properties of all data objects which have this type.

- Data objects are concrete instances of data types. Each data object has a particular type and requires all appropriate storage space. User defined data types can be created by using TYPES statement. They can be either elementary or structured.

- User defined data types allow you to create all application specific type universes. This structure can be defined centrally and thus made known to the ABAP/4 programming environment.

3.2 Data Fields

SAP R/3 Requirements:

- ABAP/4 variable names can be a maximum of 30 characters long for DATA fields as applicable.

- SELECT-OPTIONS and PARAMETERS can be a maximum of 8 characters long.

- On selection screen for reports, SELECT-OPTIONS field must be defined FOR table that appears as CheckTable within the field definition (eg WERKS must be defined as S_WERKS FOR T001W-WERKS').

Standards:

All variables should be defined by using the type declared in the TYPE pool.

When custom variables have a corresponding SAP variable, use the name that reflects that particular SAP data element or field name. Do not use variable names containing '-'.as they can be confused with table fields. Underscores should be used to separate words contained in variable/constant names. In addition, make the names descriptive.

For program readability and maintainability, remove defined fields that are never referenced and code which can never be logically executed. Whenever possible, the LIKE parameter should be used to define work fields.

Format:

X_	X(28)
	Sample -

Position	Description	Values	Meaning
1-2	Variable Description	C_	for Constants
		P_	for Parameters
		S_	for Select-Options
		R_	for ranges
		V_	for Global Variables
		ty_	Types
		it_	for Global Internal Tables
		wa_	for Global Work Areas
		def_	for Define
		<g_fs>	for Global Field-Symbols
		L_	for Local Variable
		l_it_	for Local Internal Tables
		l_wa_	for Local Work Areas
		<l_fs>	for Local Field-Symbols
		fp_v_	for variables parameters used in Subroutines (FORM)
		fp_wa_	for work areas parameters used in Subroutines (FORM)

		fp_it_	for tables parameters used in Subroutines (FORM)
3/4-30	Freely Definable		use abbreviations for clear and Concise names.

3.3   Abbreviations

When defining Data Fields, use clear and understandable names. It is important that abbreviations are used consistently in all names. To determine an abbreviation for a word, strip out all vowels and insignificant characters. Names that begin with a vowel retain the vowel in the abbreviation. Add vowels back in when abbreviations for two different names are alike. Abbreviations will be based on English names.

CHAPTER 4

ABAP/4 Dictionary

When creating a custom table, carefully plan its design and structure. Define the table fields appropriately. Always place the key fields at the front of the record layout. Use the SAP database administrator to help to design the table and its attributes, index, and buffer settings.

4.1 Tables

When defining custom tables always place the key fields at the front of the record structure.

4.1.1 HANA Tables

SAP HANA Information Modeler; also known as HANA Data Modeler is heart of HANA System. It enables to create modeling views at the top of database tables & implement business logic to create a meaningful report for analysis.

Features of Information Modeler

- Provides multiple views of transactional data stored in physical tables of HANA database for analysis & business logic purpose.

- Informational modeler only works for column based storage table(s).

- Information Modeling Views are consumed by Java or HTML based applications or SAP tools like, SAP Lumira or Analysis Office for reporting purpose.

- Also possible to use third party tools like MS Excel to connect to HANA and create reports as applicable.

- SAP HANA Modeling Views exploit real power of SAP HANA as applicable.

There are three types of Information Views, defined as:

- Attribute View
- Analytic View
- Calculation View

Attribute View

Attributes are non-measurable elements in a database table. They represent master data & similar to characteristics of BW. Attribute Views are dimensions in a database or are used to join dimensions or other attribute views in modeling.

Important features are:

- Attribute views are used in Analytic and Calculation views.
- Attribute view represent master data.
- Used to filter size of dimension tables in Analytic and Calculation View.

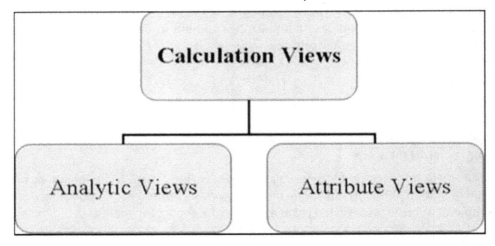

Ref: tutorialspoint

Characteristics of Attribute View

- Attribute Views in HANA are used to join Dimension tables or other Attribute Views.
- Attribute Views are used in Analytical and Calculation Views for analysis to pass master data.
- They are similar to Characteristics in BM and contain master data.
- Attribute Views are used for performance optimization in large size Dimension tables, you can limit the number of attributes in an Attribute View which are further used for Reporting and analysis purpose.
- Attribute Views are used to model master data to give some context.

Analytic View

Analytic Views use power of SAP HANA to perform calculations and aggregation functions on the tables in database. It has at least one fact table that has measures and primary keys of dimension tables and surrounded by dimension tables contain master data.

Important features are:

- Analytic views are designed to perform Star schema queries.
- Analytic views contain at least one fact table and multiple dimension tables with master data and perform calculations and aggregations
- They are similar to Info Cubes and Info objects in SAP BW.
- Analytic views can be created on the top of Attribute views and Fact tables and performs calculations like number of unit sold, total price, etc.

Characteristics of Analytic View

Following are the properties of SAP HANA Analytic View:

- Analytic Views are used to perform complex calculations and Aggregate functions like Sum, Count, Min, Max, Etc.
- Analytic Views are designed to run Start schema queries.
- Each Analytic View has one Fact table surrounded by multiple dimension tables. Fact table contains primary key for each Dim table and measures.
- Analytic Views are similar to Info Objects and Info sets of SAP BW.

Calculation Views

Calculation Views are used on the top of Analytic and Attribute views to perform complex calculations, which are not possible with Analytic Views. Calculation view is a combination of base column tables, Attribute views and Analytic views to provide business logic.

Important features are:

- Calculation Views are defined either graphical by using HANA Modeling feature or scripted in the SQL.
- It is created to perform complex calculations, which are not possible with other views- Attribute and Analytic views of SAP HANA modeler.
- One or more Attribute views and Analytic views are consumed with help of inbuilt functions like Projects, Union, Join, Rank in a Calculation View.

Characteristics of Calculation View

Below given are few characteristics of Calculation Views:

- Calculation Views are used to consume Analytic, Attribute and other Calculation Views.
- They are used to perform complex calculations, which are not possible with other Views.
- There are two ways to create Calculation Views- SQL Editor or Graphical Editor.
- Built-in Union, Join, Projection & Aggregation nodes.

Fact and Dimension Table

Fact Table contains Primary Keys for Dimension table and measures. They are joined with Dimension tables in HANA Views to meet business logic.

Example of Measures: Number of unit sold, Total Price, Average Delay time, etc.

Dimension Table contains master data and is joined with one or more fact tables to make some business logic. Dimension tables are used to create schemas with fact tables and can be normalized.

Example of Dimension Table: Customer, Product, etc.

Suppose a company sells products to customers. Every sale is a fact that happens within the company and the fact table is used to record these facts.

Schemas are logical description of tables in Data Warehouse. Schemas are created by joining multiple fact and Dimension tables to meet some business logic.

Database uses relational model to store data. However, Data Warehouse use Schemas that join dimensions and fact tables to meet business logic. There are three types of Schemas used in a Data Warehouse:

- Star Schema
- Snowflakes Schema
- Galaxy Schema

Star Schema

In Star Schema, Each Dimension is joined to one single Fact table. Each Dimension is represented by only one dimension and is not further normalized.

Dimension Table contains set of attribute that are used to analyze the data.

Example:

In example given below, we have a Fact table FactSales that has Primary keys for all the Dim tables and measures units_sold and dollars_ sold to do analysis.

Snowflakes Schema

In Snowflakes schema, some of Dimension tables are further, normalized and Dim tables are connected to single Fact Table. Normalization is used to organize attributes and tables of database to minimize the data redundancy.

Normalization involves breaking a table into less redundant smaller tables without losing any information and smaller tables are joined to Dimension table.

Galaxy Schema

In Galaxy Schema, there are multiple Fact tables and Dimension tables. Each Fact table stores primary keys of few Dimension tables and measures/facts to do analysis.

4.1.1.1 Row Data Storage vs. Column Data Storage

Relational databases typically use row-based data storage. However Column-based storage is more suitable for many business applications. SAP HANA supports both row-based and column-based storage, and is particularly optimized for column-based storage.

As shown in the figure below, a database table is conceptually a two-dimensional structure composed of cells arranged in rows and columns.

Because computer memory is structured linearly, there are two options for the sequences of cell values stored in contiguous memory locations:

Row Storage – It stores table records in a sequence of rows.
Column Storage – It stores table records in a sequence of columns i.e. the entries of a column is stored in contiguous memory locations.

Table

	Country	Product	Sales
Row 1	India	Chocolate	1000
Row 2	India	Ice-cream	2000
Row 3	Germany	Chocolate	4000
Row 4	US	Noodle	500

Row Store

Row 1	India
	Chocolate
	1000
Row 2	India
	Ice-cream
	2000
Row 3	Germany
	Chocolate
	4000
Row 4	US
	Noodle
	500

Column Store

Country	India
	India
	Germany
	US
Product	Chocolate
	Ice-cream
	Chocolate
	Noodle
Sales	1000
	2000
	4000
	500

Traditional databases store data simply in rows. The HANA in-memory database stores data in both rows and columns. It is this combination of both storage approaches that produces the speed, flexibility and performance of the HANA database.

Row Store

Order	Customer	Currency	Amount
456	JaTeCo	EUR	1300
457	SAP	EUR	750
458	Sorali	EUR	115
459	SAP	EUR	30.000

```
SELECT *  ....
  WHERE ORDER = 457
```
Good performance

```
SELECT SUM(Amount)...
```
Low performance

Column Store

Order	Customer	Currency	Amount
456	JaTeCo	EUR	1300
457	SAP	EUR	750
458	Sorali	EUR	115
459	SAP	EUR	30.000

```
SELECT *  ....
  WHERE ORDER = 457
```
Low performance

```
SELECT SUM(Amount)...
```
Good performance

4.1.1.2 Advantages of column-based tables:

Faster Data Access:

Only affected columns have to be read during the selection process of a query. Any of the columns can serve as an index.

Better Compression:

Columnar data storage allows highly efficient compression because the majority of the columns contain only few distinct values (compared to number of rows).

Better parallel Processing:

In a column store, data is already vertically partitioned. This means that operations on different columns can easily be processed in parallel. If multiple columns need to be searched or aggregated, each of these operations can be assigned to a different processor core

4.1.1.3 Advantages and disadvantages of row-based tables:

Row based tables have advantages in the following circumstances:

- The application needs to only process a single record at one time (many selects and/or updates of single records).
- The application typically needs to access a complete record (or row).
- Neither aggregations nor fast searching are required.
- The table has a small number of rows (e. g. configuration tables, system tables).

Row based tables have disadvantages in the following circumstances:

In case of analytic applications where aggregation are used and fast search and processing is required. In row based tables all data in a row has to be read even though the requirement may be to access data from a few columns.

4.1.1.4 Which type of tables should be preferred – Row-based or Column-based?

When to Use Row Storage?

Row storage is more suitable for tables

- that contain mainly distinct values
  → low compression rate

- in which most/all columns are relevant

- that are not subject to aggregation or search operations on non-indexed columns

- that are fully buffered

- that have a small number of records

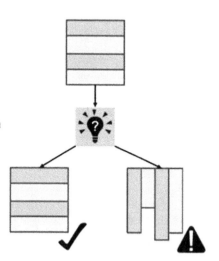

When to Use Columnar Storage?

Columnar storage is best for tables

- that are subject to column operations on a large number of rows

- that have a large number of columns, more unused

- that are subject to aggregations and intensive search operations

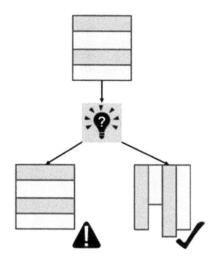

Column Store Dictionary Compression

Logical Table					Dictionary		Compressed column		Inverted index	
Order	Customer	Currency	Amount							
456	JaTeCo	EUR	1300		1	JaTeCo	1	1	1	1
457	SAP	EUR	750		2	PicoBit	2	3	2	5,7
458	Sorali	EUR	115		3	SAP	3	5	3	2,4,8
459	SAP	EUR	30.000		4	Siwusa	4	3	4	6
460	PicoBit	EUR	300		5	Sorali	5	2	5	3
461	Siwusha	EUR	600		5 entries →		6	4	Which orders	
462	PicoBit	EUR	600		3 bits to encode		7	2	of SAP?	
463	SAP	EUR	1.200				8	3		
...	...	...	...				...	...	Where is	
									order 460?	

In case of analytic applications where aggregations are used and fast search and processing is required row-based storage are not good. In row based tables all data in a row has to be read even though the requirement may be to access data from a few columns. Hence these queries on huge amounts of data take a lot of time.

In columnar tables, this information is stored physically next to each other, significantly increasing the speed of certain data queries.

The following example shows the different usage of column and row storage, and positions them relative to row and column queries. Column storage is most useful for OLAP queries (queries using any SQL aggregate functions) because these queries get just a few attributes from every data entry. But for traditional OLTP queries (queries does not use any SQL aggregate functions), it is more advantageous to store all attributes side-by-side in row tables. HANA combines the benefits of both row- and column-storage table.

Table - SALES

	Date	Country	Product	Sales
Row 1	2013-01-01	India	Chocolate	1000
Row 2	2013-01-10	India	Ice-cream	2000
Row 3	2013-02-20	Germany	Chocolate	4000
Row 4	2013-03-01	US	Noodle	500

Column Operation: SELECT SUM(SALES) FROM SALES WHERE DATE > 2012-01-01

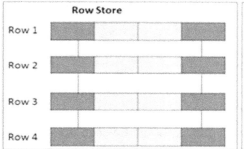
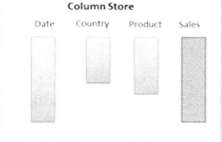

Row Operation: SELECT * FROM SALES WHERE COUNTRY = 'INDIA'

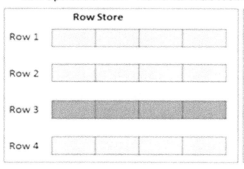
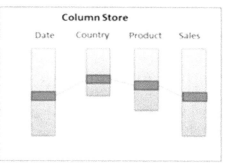

Conclusion:

To enable fast on-the-fly aggregations, ad-hoc reporting, and to benefit from compression mechanisms it is recommended that transaction data is stored in a column-based table.

The SAP HANA data-base allows joining row-based tables with column-based tables. However, it is more efficient to join tables that are located in the same row or column store. For example, master data that is frequently joined with transaction data should also be stored in column-based tables.

Dictionary: Maintain Technical Settings

✏ ⁞ 🔓 Revised<->Active 🔢

Name		Transparent Table
Short Descript.		
Last Changed		
Status	Actv.	Saved

General Properties — DB-Specific Properties

Storage Type

⦿ Column Store   ○ Row Store   ○ Undefined

4.1.2 Transparent Tables

When creating custom tables, Transparent Tables should be used in most cases. The structure of a Transparent table inside SAP is identical to its structure at the database level. Therefore the table can be accessed by both internal and external applications. All updates to SAP Tables should be performed within SAP.

4.1.3 View Tables

Use VIEW tables to join related tables that are taking large amounts of time to select from. A database View is not physically stored, but is a table derived from multiple tables. Database Views allow fields from several tables to be accessed in one view. Generally, accessing a database view is faster than selecting tables individually.

4.1.4 Index

The purpose of an Index is to quicken the scanning process when searching for specific records in a table. An Index is a copy of a table reduced to particular sorted fields to enable faster access to needed data.

- Only include fields in an index if they free the selected data significantly.

- As indexes are adjusted each time table contents are changed, create secondary indexes discerningly to minimize the impact on the system.

- When SELECTing data from a table, look at the structure of all of the available indexes and tailor the WHERE clause to take advantage of the most selective index. Use all fields in the WHERE clause for an index, as skipping one field

ruins the index.

- Place the most "common" columns at the beginning of an index. The most "common" columns are those where reports are selecting columns with no ranges - the WHERE clause for these columns is an "equal to" expression. Rearrange columns of an index to match the selection criteria. For example, if a SELECT statement is written to include columns 1 and 2 with "equal to" expressions in the WHERE clause and column 3 and 4 are selected with value ranges, then the index should be created with columns in the sequence of 1, 2, 3, 4.

- Place Columns toward the end of the index if they are either infrequently used in SELECTS or are part of reporting SELECTS that involve ranges of values.

- Be sure to order the columns in the WHERE clause of a SELECT in the same order as an index table.

- Remove unused indexes or ones that change due to report design changes.

Caution:

The creation of an index can affect performance adversely. The most suitable index for the select criteria might not be the index chosen for use by the database optimizer. Creating Indexes should be done carefully and jointly with the SAP Database Administrator. Validate the use of table indexes by performing a SQL Trace.

4.1.5 Matchcodes

Matchcodes are used to help users search for particular data records via certain non-key fields. Matchcode creation involves three separate objects:

1. Matchcode Object

Matchcodes are used as efficient secondary access paths when keys are unknown, for example as search aids when any entry field calls for an object's key but only certain other (non-key) fields of the object are known.

2. Matchcode ID's

A Matchcode ID provides a link between the field on-screen and a Matchcode Field. A selection condition can be assigned to each matchcode ID. Note: Matchcode ID's are designated as a 1 character name, and the matchcode must always be realized using index and database views.

3. Matchcode usage

Matchcode should be used for all fields that have large amount of data to be searched.

Examples:

MATNR	-	Material Number
LIFNR	-	Vendor Number
CLASS	-	Class

4.1.6 KUNNR-Customer Number Matchcode vs. Index

The following are a few of the differences between Indexes and Matchcodes that need to be considered during development:

- Matchcodes can have fields from more than one table. An Index pertains to only one table.
- Matchcode restriction is possible with selection conditions.
- Matchcodes can work as an aid in the help system.

4.1.7 Table Buffering

Database tables can be stored locally on each application server. Performance time may be improved because reading from the buffer avoids directly accessing the database. Within SAP, only POOLED and TRANSPARENT tables allow buffering. The decision to buffer a table must be made by the SAP Database Administrator.

Considerations:

- Only buffer a table that has read-only accesses made against it and is referenced frequently.
- Only buffer tables that are modifiable, if write access occurs infrequently. Changes to buffered tables get automatically logged in the database and are transferred to the application servers at regular intervals. If buffered tables are modified frequently, the additional processing needed may cancel any performance gains attained by buffering.

4.2   TYPE-GROUP

SAP R/3 Requirements:

User-defined data types are combined together in Type Groups, which can contain both type definitions and constants definitions.

Considerations:

As user-defined data types help make programs easier to read, each program should have a Type Pool and variables defined to the program should refer to those types. Overall Type Pools should be developed for each application area.

4.3   Data Type Conversion

Understanding and using data type comparisons and conversions is very important in ABAP/4. Following is a list from SAP R/3 system that lists how external data types are mapped to the ABAP/4 data types using standard domains.

External Data Type	ABAP/4 Data Type	Description
ACCP	N(6)	Posting period YYYYMM
CHAR *n*	C(*n*)	Character strings
CLNT	C(3)	Client
CUKY	C(5)	Currency key, referenced by CURR fields
CURR *n, m, s*	P((*n*+2)/2) DECIMAL *m*	Currency field, stored as DEC
DEC *n, m, s*	P((*n*+2)/2) DECIMAL *m*	Counter or amount field w/ comma & sign
DATS	D(8)	Date field (YYYYMMDD) stored as char(8)
FLTP	F(8)	Floating point number, accurate to 8 bytes
INT1	I	1-byte integer
INT2	I	2-byte integer
INT4	I	4-byte integer
LANG	C(1)	Language key
LRAW	X(*n*)	Uninterpreted sequence of bytes
LCHR	C(*n*)	Long character string, requires preceding INT2 field
NUMC *n*	N(*n*)	Character field with only digits
QUAN *n, m, s*	P((*n*+2)/2) DECIMAL *m*	Quantity field, points to a unit field with format UNIT
RAW *n*	X(*n*)	Long byte string needs preceding INT2 field
TIMS	T(6)	Time field (hhmmss), stored as char(6)
UNIT	C(*n*)	Unit key for QUAN fields
VARC *n*	C(*n*)	Long character string, not supported from Release 3.0
n: no. of places	*m*: number of decimal places.	*s*: sign flag

Considerations:

- When non-standard conversions are needed to display differently from SAP's internal format or vice-versa, create a Conversion Exit for the Domain. This should be done by creating two function modules placed in the same function group.

  ◊ one module to convert from display format to internal format.

  ◊ the other to convert from internal format to the external format.

- Data types of P and I are treated the same on all SAP supported platforms.

- Note that floating points have an accuracy up to 15 decimal places on all platforms, and that the rounding behavior may change. SAP advises that when two floating point numbers need to be tested for equality, that the difference be very small.

- Use program RSANAL00 to execute conversions by an ABAP.

CHAPTER 5

Security Authorizations Considerations

5.1   Requests/tasks

When an object is changed, the system automatically asks for a short description and then creates 2 levels:

- Transportable request
- Developments/correction task

The description is copied to both levels, please remember to maintain both levels when changing. The documentation should make clear what has been changed, not only from a programmer's point of view, but also from a more general point of view. Be specific about how things worked before and after the change.

5.2   Authorization checks in program

Since the SELECT statement does not perform any authorization checks, you must program these yourself with AUTHORITY-CHECK. By doing this, you can protect any functions and objects in the R/3 System from unauthorized access. If you are doing any UPDATE/ADD on a table, you must use this technique. You must also check this with the Security Administrator. Always use AUTHORITY-CHECK.

- Every executable program to be assigned to a transaction code.
- Ensure that all custom ABAP programs that may be submitted / executed must be attached to a transaction code. An ABAP program which has been attached to a transaction code, an authority check on the specific transaction code must be inserted at the beginning of the ABAP program
- Authorization checks in custom transactions must be referenced in SU24. This also applies to table maintenance transactions (SM30 variants).
- Ensure that SAP user-ids/user groups are never hardcoded into ABAP programs.

5.3 Authorization checks for reports

All reports must be allocated to a transaction code, for security reasons, it is given by responsible for reports.

5.4 Authorizations linked to TRANSACTIONS

Next to transactions designed for business purposes, transactions have to be created in order to allow online start of reports (as SA38 and ABAP transactions will not be allowed in Production), as well as for table maintenance.

The authorization objects checked within transactions have to be recorded via transaction SU24. Both SAP objects and custom objects need to be assigned to the transaction.

5.5 Authorizations linked to Custom Tables

Two types of custom tables have to be differenciated. Difference is base on the table attributes :

- Delivery class
- Customizing table (del.class :C)
- Application table (del.class :A)

Customizing tables :

Maintenance performed via standard transactions. These tables are not maintained in the production environment but data is to be transported .

These tables have to be linked to the IMG (under KFI configuration)

Application tables :

A maintenance transaction is to be created for each custom application table. Authorization control needs to be performed within the maintenance transaction for all relevant organizational elements (part of the table key).

Next to these checks a global control on the transaction object (S_TCODE) is performed and also checks using authorization object S_TABU_DIS with necessary authorization group.

Note: It is recommended always for customizable tables maintained by users in the landscape to have organization parameter part of table definition and use this org parameter to maintain authorizations on maintenance events.

CHAPTER 6

ABAP/4
Coding Techniques

6.1   Internal Tables

An Internal Table is a group of records created at runtime. **It is mandatory to define all internal tables using user-defined data types and without a header line.** An explicit work area for the table must be defined if loop processing will be done on this table. OCCURS is obsolete Declaration.

Example

> TYPES: begin of ty_example,
>
>   field1 type bukrs,
>
>   field2(20),
>
>   end of ty_example.
>
> DATA: it_example _TYPE HASHED TABLE OF ty_example,
>   wa_example TYPE ty_example.

6.1.1   Filling an Internal Table

6.1.1.1 Select Into

When an Internal Table needs to be created directly from one database table, use the SELECT INTO to fill the Internal Table. The contents of IT_T001 will be replaced by the selected data so a REFRESH is not needed.

Example:

SELECT * FROM T001 INTO TABLE IT_T001.

If an Internal Table is to be created directly from database tables and the contents currently in the Internal Table need to be kept, add the APPENDING TABLE parameter.

Example:

```
SELECT SINGLE * FROM T001W APPENDING TABLE IT_MARA WHERE WERKS
= V_WERKS.
```

Considerations:

- This is only relevant for Internal Tables that are as wide or wider than the database table being SELECTed.

- It is always faster to use the INTO TABLE version of a SELECT statement than to use APPEND statements.

6.1.1.2 Append

Append adds a new entry to an Internal Table. The system does not check if a record with the same key exists.

Considerations:

- As APPEND adds new entries to an Internal Table, duplicate entries may occur. If the table already contains the number of entries specified in the OCCURS parameter, the additional entries are rolled to the paging area, resulting in longer runtimes.

- When using Internal Tables with a header line, avoid unnecessary assignments to the header line. Use statements which have an explicit work area.

Example:

More Efficient
APPEND V_TAB TO IT_TAB.
Less Efficient
IT_TAB = V_TAB. APPEND IT_TAB

- As of Release 3.0C, the addition LINES OF can be added to the APPEND statement. The statement is used to add a block of lines to an Internal Table. When appropriate, use APPEND with the block command instead of APPENDING single lines during a LOOP. The block command is faster and easier to read.

Example:

More Efficient
APPEND LINES OF IT_TAB1 TO IT_TAB2.
Less Efficient
LOOP AT IT_TAB1. APPEND IT_TAB1 TO IT_TAB2 ENDLOOP.

6.1.1.3 Insert

Use INSERT to add single rows or blocks of rows to an Internal Table as a specific position.

Example:

INSERT IT_TAB INDEX 6.

Considerations:

* When a block of lines is to be inserted at a specific position, use the LINES OF parameter of the INSERT statement. INSERTING a block of lines is faster than INSERTING one row at a time during a LOOP. This example will insert rows 3 through 7 from IT_TAB1 into IT_TAB2 as rows 4, 5, 6, and line 4 from IT_TAB2 will become line 7 after the INSERT.

Example:

INSERT LINES OF IT_TAB1 FROM 3 TO 5 INTO IT_TAB2 INDEX 4.

6.1.2   Retrieving from an Internal Table

6.1.2.1 Read Table

READ TABLE is used to read a single row from an Internal Table.

READ TABLE IT_TAB is used to read a Internal Table using the Internal Table's header line as the output area.

READ TABLE IT_TAB INTO <wa> is used to read an Internal Table and use the work area as the output area.

Considerations:

- When reading a single record in an Internal Table, the READ TABLE WITH KEY is not a direct READ. Therefore, SORT the table and use READ TABLE WITH KEY BINARY SEARCH. When BINARY SEARCH is used, the system starts the search in the middle of the table. It then checks the first half or second half depending if the key fields are bigger or smaller than the middle entry.

- Specify the key fields for read access explicitly. If you do not, the key fields have to be computed dynamically by the runtime system.

Example:

More Efficient
READ TABLE IT_TAB WITH KEY K= 'X' BINARY SEARCH.

Less Efficient
MOVE SPACE TO IT_TAB. TAB-K = 'X'. READ TABLE IT_TAB BINARY SEARCH.

6.1.2.2 LOOP

LOOP ... WHERE is faster than LOOP/CHECK because LOOP ... WHERE evaluates the specified condition internally.

Example:

More Efficient
*Key access with LOOP WHERE LOOP AT TAB WHERE K = KVAL.   " ... ENDLOOP.

Less Efficient
*Key access with LOOP/CHECK LOOP AT TAB. CHECK TAB-K = KVAL.   " ... ENDLOOP.

- Make the comparison operators share a common type; as with any logical expression, the performance is better if the operands of a comparison share a common type.

- Performance can be further enhanced if the LOOP WHERE is combined with FROM i1 and/or TO i2.

6.1.3 Modifying an Internal Table

6.1.3.1 Collect

The COLLECT statement scans the Internal Table for an entry where the default key matches that of the entry in the Internal Table's header record. If a match is found, the system sums any field of type F, P, I, N in that record; if no record exists, the header record is inserted into the Internal Table. When working with Internal Tables the COLLECT statement is very CPU intensive and should be avoided. When COLLECTing on an Internal Table use the following alternative code:

```
READ TABLE  IT_TAB WITH KEY V_KEY BINARY SEARCH. CASE SY-SUBRC.
                                    WHEN 0.
                                    IT_TAB-AMT = IT_TAB-AMT + V_
NEW_AMT.                MOVE ...
 MODIFY IT_TAB INDEX SY-INDEX.                       WHEN 4.
                           MOVE ...
                    INSERT IT_TAB INDEX SY-INDEX.
WHEN 8.                                                 MOVE ...
                                         APPEND IT_TAB.
ENDCASE
```

6.1.3.2 Modify

Use the MODIFY command to change a line within an Internal Table

Example:

```
LOOP AT IT_TAB.                          MOVE
C_INITIALIZE TO IT_TAB-INITIALIZE.       MODIFY IT_TAB.
            ENDLOOP.
```

6.1.3.3 Delete

Use the DELETE command to delete a row or group of rows from an Internal Table. When DELETEing a group of rows from an Internal Table, delete them using a DELETE WHERE clause instead of a single row at a time during a LOOP, unless other activity takes place during the LOOP.

Example:

DELETE IT_TAB WERKS EQ C_0010.	W H E R E

Considerations:

- To delete all rows in an Internal Table, use the REFRESH statement.
- When working with Internal Tables that are very large, use the FREE command after the Internal Table has served its purpose and will not be used again.

Example: If Table IT_TAB is 10MB, use

FREE IT_TAB.

If an Internal Table is defined locally in a subroutine, the allocated memory is released upon completion of the subroutine, so the REFRESH statement is not needed.

6.1.4   Sorting Internal Tables

Qualify all SORT statements with the BY option and limit the sorting of data to fields that must be used to satisfy the requirements. SORTs, in general, are expensive.

Considerations:

- Be aware of the effect on character sequence using SORT.
    - ◊ Upper case characters can be sorted before lower case letters or, lower case can be sorted before upper case.
    - ◊ The sort might place letters before numbers or vice versa.
- SORTED Internal Tables
    - ◊ When SORTing Internal Tables, specify the fields to be SORTed.

Example:

More Efficient
SORT IT_TAB BY FLD1 FLD2
Less Efficient
SORT IT_TAB.

   ◊   Building SORTED Tables

If the amount of data is less than 20 entries, or if read access to the Internal Table is needed while the ITAB is being filled, use a one-step approach using

READ/INSERT. If the data amount is larger and read-access is only needed to the completely filled table, use the two-step process.

Example:

One-step Approach: READ/INSERT

* I_DEST is filled with 1000 entries
REFRESH I_DEST.
LOOP AT TAB_SRC.
  READ TABLE I_DEST WITH KEY K = TAB_SRC-K BINARY SEARCH.
  INSERT TAB_SRC INTO I_DEST INDEX SY-TABIX.
ENDLOOP.
Use on small tables

Two-step Approach: APPEND, SORT
* I_DEST is filled with 1000 entries REFRESH I_DEST. LOOP AT TAB_SRC. APPEND TAB_SRC TO I_DEST. ENDLOOP. SORT TAB_DEST BY K. *Use on large tables*

6.1.5   General Internal Table Techniques

6.1.5.1 DESCRIBE

DESCRIBE determines the number of entries in an Internal Table.

Example:

More Efficient
DESCRIBE TABLE IT_TAB LINES V_LNE_CNTR
Less Efficient
LOOP AT IT_TAB. V_LNE_CNTR = V_LNE_CNT + 1. ENDLOOP

6.1.5.2 RANGES

The RANGES statement creates Internal Tables that have the structure of a SELECT-OPTION table, but the RANGES do not have the same functionality.

As a standard, when an Internal Table is to be used as above, use the TYPE RANGE OF to define the range. The declaration of a ranges table with the statement RANGES is obsolete.

Example:

Standard
DATA: r_tab type range of lfb1-bukrs.
Obsolete
RANGES R_tab for lfb1-Bukrs
Non-Standard
DATA: BEGIN OF I_TAB, OCCURS nn,
SIGN(1),
OPTION(2),
LOW LIKE ......,
HIGH LIKE ......,
END OF I_TAB.

As a standard, when using the IN operator in combination with SUBMIT, SELECT, CHECK, WHILE, or IF, always define the associated Internal Table using SELECT-OPTIONS or RANGES Never define the selection criteria in an Internal Table directly. Using RANGES will make for easier maintainability, readability, and conforms to SAP recommendations.

Considerations when using RANGES:

- It is not allowed to declare internal tables with header lines. Due to this, the statement RANGES is not allowed in header lines. To declare a ranges-table, you can use the addition TYPE|LIKE RANGE OF

- RANGES are not select screen fields.

- RANGES are not passed to the logical database programs.

- RANGES do not support the short form of logical expressions,

Example:

CHECK R_BUKRS is incorrect.

- RANGES are to be used in the WHERE clause of OPEN SQL statements in expressions with the IN parameter.

- RANGES dynamically filled with large amount of data (e.g. 10,000 entries) should not be used within SELECT as they fail at run time with ORACLE errors. The following example illustrates this:

Example:

```
select mblnr mjahr matnr
    from  mseg
    into  table it_mseg
    where matnr in r_matnr.
```

Problem can be avoided by doing SELECT within a loop and changing the RANGE to an internal table.

Example:

```
loop at it_matnr.
    select mblnr mjahr matnr
      from  mseg
      appending table it_mseg
      where matnr = it_matnr-matnr.
      endloop.
```

6.1.5.3 Miscellaneous

- Use the FREE statement to release the memory allocated to Internal Tables. The FREE statement should follow the last statement used to process the data in the table. Use the FREE statement where you no longer need the internal table in your program.

As noted above in APPEND, when using Internal Tables with a header line, avoid unnecessary assignments to the header line. Use statements that have an explicit work area:

Examples:

More Efficient
APPEND V_WA TO IT_TAB.

Less Efficient
MOVE V_WA TO IT_TAB. APPEND IT_TAB.

More Efficient
INSERT V_WA INTO IT_TAB.

Less Efficient
MOVE V_WA TO IT_TAB.
INSERT IT_TAB.

More Efficient
COLLECT V_WA INTO IT_TAB.

Less Efficient
MOVE V_WA TO IT_TAB.
COLLECT IT_TAB.

- When performing control break logic on Internal Tables and FIELD-GROUPS, make use of the AT NEW, AT END OF, ON CHANGE OF, and SUM commands. The use of ABAP's control break commands will provide easier readability and maintainability versus coding the break logic without the benefit of the commands.

6.1.6   FIELD GROUPS

SAP R/3 Requirements:

FIELD-GROUPS combines several existing fields together under one name. Used in conjunction with INSERT, EXTRACT, and LOOP. Conceptually, it is similar to processing Internal Tables.

Considerations:

- FIELD-GROUP are no longer necessary in SAP R/3 3.0. Given the improvements in memory management of 3.0, internal tables are considered more efficient than FIELD-GROUPS.

- As soon as the first dataset for a FIELD-GROUP has been extracted with EXTRACT, the FIELD-GROUP can no longer be extended with INSERT.

- FIELD-GROUPS can only have records added to them before a sort or loop command is performed.

6.2   Logical Database

In most cases, it is likely that coding database retrievals with SELECT statements will prove more efficient than using a Logical Database (LDB) program. A LDB program reads tables with nested SELECT loops. The depth of the SELECT into the LDB hierarchy depends on the GET statement in the ABAP corresponding to the tables located at the lowest level of the LDB hierarchy. If a program does not need information from a superior table in the hierarchy, unnecessary reads will occur. Before using a LDB, be sure the logic cannot be coded more efficiently using SELECT.

The Logical Database allows reading of hierarchically related tables using GET statements. The advantages of the logical databases are:

- Ease of programming

- Selection screen and filtering of the data

- Authorization checking

If a LDB is chosen, the most efficient logical database possible should be used. Study the selection criteria and which secondary indexes are used for that view. Provide the appropriate selection criteria to limit the number of database reads. Force users to provide selection criteria by evaluating the selection criteria entered on the selection screen during AT SELECTION-SCREEN event. Use Matchcodes for selection and report sorting.

Considerations:

- Access to database information via GET provides automatic security checking and checking on key fields from the selection screen. The SELECT statement will require both of these operations to be coded.

- When getting information from a hierarchy database via a logical database view, the order in which you check statements is important. Attempt to eliminate any data which is not required at the earliest stage possible.

- An ABAP/4 report can work with only one logical database, but every logical database can be shared by several reports.

- When using a logical database, the selection screen of the report is called automatically by the logical database program. When using the SELECT statements the selection screen must be programmed.

- Even if a logical database will not be attached to your ABAP/4 Report, transaction SE36 is useful to learn. - especially the secondary index tables and relationships between tables.

- Logical Database Programs cannot be attached to Function Modules.

- When using Logical Databases, you must take into consideration the following:

    - ✓ Determine if some of the selection screen fields can be required fields. This would force the users to put in a value into these fields limiting the number of rows retrieved within the logical database program. The selection screen can be dynamically modified by the program using the logical database and using AT SELECTION-SCREEN output event.

✓ Use the GET dbtab <fields>... option to retrieve only the fields needed by your program. This option requires the initialization event to populate all internal tables with the table name and the field name. Use help on GET for additional information.

6.3 Subroutines

The three subroutine alternatives are:

- FORM routines
- Include programs
- Call functions

Calling ABAP/4 subroutines can create conflicts between the goals of transparency, maintainability and performance. In each individual case, consider the following:

- How often is the form called?
- How much time is required by the respective module call?
- The guideline values for resource consumption:

Subroutine Type	Microseconds
Internal PERFORM	3
External PERFORM	20-50
CALL FUNCTION	20-100
CALL DIALOG	10,000-150,000

6.3.1 Forms

FORMS are subroutines that allow a programmer to define a process once in a program and call that routine from different places within the program or from other programs. A FORM should be used for large coding blocks. Common sections of code accessed from several points in an ABAP should also be put into FORMS.

If a block of code is executed more than once, it should be placed in a subroutine at the bottom of the code. This makes the code more readable, requires less indentation, and is easier to debug since the debugger can jump through an entire subroutine via a PF key.

For good modularization, the decision of whether or not to PERFORM a subroutine should be made before the subroutine is called.

Example:

More Efficient
IF f1 NE 0.   **PERFORM sub1.** **ENDIF.** **FORM sub1.** **.......** **ENDFORM.**
Less Efficient

PERFORM sub1.
FORM sub1.
IF f1 NE 0.
  EXIT.
  ENDIF.
ENDFORM..

Considerations:

- Don't use PERFORM<form name>(<program name>) unnecessarily. Overall runtime will be increased because the entire program containing the actual perform must be loaded into memory.

- Subroutines should be limited to one page of printed source code.

- For manageability, subroutines should be created with the concept of a "black box" in mind. The routine will have certain input and output parameters, and knowledge of the parameters should be sufficient to use the routine. Subroutines should not, as a rule, reference global data. Alterations made to global data within the black box produce less manageable code.

- Calling a subroutine without parameters requires minimal extra CPU time. The more parameters passed, the more CPU time a subroutine call requires. Passing by reference requires less CPU time than passing by value. The amount of CPU time required to pass a single parameter by value is dependent on the size (field length) of the parameter.

- Formal parameters must be fully typed.

6.3.2 Includes

An INCLUDE is a section of code which has been separated due to program size or it is in common use by several programs. Effective use of includes can reduce development and maintenance time.

Consideration:

A program that uses include incorporates it at generation time, so if the include is altered all the programs that use it must be re-generated. SAP has to regenerate if the last update date and the regeneration date of the program are not the same.

6.3.3 Function Modules

For speed, internal routines are the fastest. Functions should be used for general routines so maintenance can be performed collectively. The routines are loaded into a buffer so their first access is very slow. The most frequently accessed functions are held sequentially in memory, and as new routines are used the least frequent routines are dropped.

For speed internal routines are quicker than Functions. Create function calls discerningly. Perform does not require the 'load' of includes, etc. that call functions do. Therefore, create function calls when code is used by multiple programs, otherwise use perform.

Consideration:

- A Function module and the calling program have separate work areas. The separated work area means there is no data interface between the function module and the calling program. They are limited to the passing of import and export parameters. This improves abstraction and manageability at the cost of efficiency.

- A CALL to a Function Module causes the loading of the entire Function Group. Therefore, always limit the number of function modules within a group to less than five.

6.3.4 Submit, Call, Leave To

The commands SUBMIT and SUBMIT AND RETURN can be used to start another report and CALL and LEAVE TO can be used to start another transaction. These commands can be very useful to build integrated functions.

Considerations:

- Commands which "go back" after execution use additional ROLL area, therefore, to protect system performance; complete one SUBMIT…. AND RETURN prior to initiating another.

- LEAVE TO cannot be used in a transaction using BDC processing.

6.4   SQL

6.4.1   ABAP/4 Open SQL

The SAP programming language ABAP/4 has its own dialect of SQL. This is a rudimentary SQL language designed for database compatibility and independence. The design philosophy was to reduce SQL functionality to such a level that code written using ABAP/4 OPEN SQL was suitable for execution against all of the major databases used by SAP, thus improving portability.

- When using the SELECT statement, study the key and always provide as much of the left-most part of the key as possible. If the entire key can be qualified, code a SELECT SINGLE not just a SELECT

- Order the columns in the WHERE clause in the same order as the key.

- Avoid the use of LIKE with a pattern in an ABAP/4 OPEN SQL statement when accessing a large table. It is less efficient and can cause scanning of the table.

- Fields that are compared in SELECT statements should have similar attributes. If they don't, then the system will have to convert the data every time a comparison is made. When the data fields can't be matched via table definitions, move the data to a temporary field in the program before doing the compare (if you will be using the same field for several comparisons)

- Familiarize yourself with the data being processed before using the SELECT statement. Table types greatly influence how the ABAP/4 program should process the data.

- When using ABAP/4 OPEN SQL, the user is restricted to data pertaining to the client they are currently logged into unless the table is client independent or "client-specified" is used.

- When SELECTing data from a table, look at the structure of all of the available indexes and tailor the WHERE clause to take advantage of the most selective index.

6.4.1.1 SELECTING from HANA Column store Tables

When selecting from a HANA column store table, always provide list of table columns required for further processing. Always qualify the SELECT statement as fully as possible with the WHERE option. This allows the database to evaluate the table columns and return only the records matching the selection criteria.

If aggregations on the data are required, mention aggregations during the SELECT statement. Avoid doing aggregate calculations after data selection and import into internal tables.

Try to shift processing of data from Application Server to Database Server wherever possible. Use join conditions in SELECT statement instead of multiple SELECT statements with FOR ALL entries operation.

In the classical databases approach, internal tables with FOR ALL ENTRIES has been used extensively to reduce load on database server and bring the load onto Application server. This is no more required with HANA. In any case, data selections have to be done with proper analysis of the requirements and framing the selection.

Use ABAP managed database procedures wherever required to take advantage of the in-memory computing capabilities of HANA.

Implications of an In-Memory Database

In-memory computing imperative:

- Avoid (unnecessary) movement of large data volume
- Perform data-intensive calculations in the database

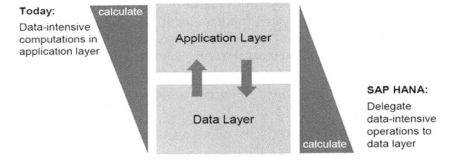

Today:
Data-intensive computations in application layer

calculate

Application Layer

Data Layer

calculate

SAP HANA:
Delegate data-intensive operations to data layer

6.4.1.2 ABAP Managed Database Procedures (AMDP) on HANA

ABAP Managed Database Procedures are a new feature in AS ABAP allowing developers to write database procedures directly in ABAP. You can think of a Database Procedure as a function stored and executed in the database. The implementation language varies from one database system to another. In SAP HANA it is SQL Script. Using AMDP allows developers to create and execute those database procedures in the ABAP environment using ABAP methods and ABAP data types

Why should I use them?

As you can imagine (and hopefully have already experienced) calculations executed while retrieving the data from the database can significant reduce the runtime of an ABAP program. Especially when the calculations can be parallelized.

Using SQL and all of its possibilities is one example of this. But this has limitations. A SQL statement always has one result set and the calculation must be done in one single step. If you have complex calculations which you want to execute on the database you need other possibilities. In those cases and many more, database procedures come into the game. And the vehicle of choice to implement database procedures as an ABAP geek are AMDPs.

How do I create an AMDP?

Creating an AMDP is as easy as it can get in ABAP. You can simply implement SQLScript in an ABAP method:

```
METHOD <meth> BY DATABASE PROCEDURE
  FOR <db>
  LANGUAGE <db_lang>
  [OPTIONS <db_options>]
  [USING <db_entities>].

  < Insert SQLScript code here >

ENDMETHOD.
```

Also important to know is that every class containing an AMDP must contain the interface IF_AMDP_MARKER_HDB. But that's all – You don't need anything else.

Example:

Here we go – a very very simple example but it should give you an idea. A real life example is of course much more complex and normally has more in- and/or output parameters.

```
 1  CLASS ZCL_DEMO_AMDP DEFINITION PUBLIC.
 2
 3    PUBLIC SECTION.
 4      INTERFACES if_amdp_marker_hdb .
 5
 6      TYPES: BEGIN OF ty_output,
 7               company_name TYPE snwd_bpa-company_name,
 8             END OF ty_output,
 9             tt_output TYPE STANDARD TABLE OF ty_output.
10
11      METHODS my_method
12        IMPORTING
13          VALUE(iv_number) TYPE i
14        EXPORTING
15          VALUE(et_top)    TYPE tt_output .
16  ENDCLASS.
17
18  CLASS ZCL_DEMO_AMDP IMPLEMENTATION.
19
20    METHOD my_method BY DATABASE PROCEDURE FOR HDB
21                     LANGUAGE SQLSCRIPT OPTIONS READ-ONLY
22                     USING snwd_bpa.
23      -- SQL Script coding
24      et_top = select top :iv_number company_name from snwd_bpa;
25    ENDMETHOD.
26  ENDCLASS.
```

In this example we have created a database procedure for SAP HANA (FOR HDB) using SQLScript (LANGUAGE SQLSCRIPT) which simply selects the company name for our top business partners. The number of business partners to be selected is passed as an input parameter (iv_number) which is used in the SQL Script statement.

6.4.1.3 Core Data Services (CDS) Views on HANA

With the availability of the SAP HANA platform there has been a paradigm shift in the way business applications are developed at SAP. The rule-of-thumb is simple: *Do as much as you can in the database to get the best performance*. This is also true for the underlying data models of the business applications.

CDS provides enhanced view building capabilities to enable you to easily define semantically rich and re-useable data models in the database. The new view building features include new join types, new clauses as well as support for aggregate functions and SQL functions. All these features are "open". The features are provided in a new text editor for DDL sources in ADT 2.19.

CDS simplifies and harmonizes the way you define and consume your data models, regardless of the consumption technology. Technically, it is an enhancement of SQL which provides you with a data definition language (DDL) for defining semantically rich database tables/views (CDS entities) and user-defined types in the database. The enhancements include:

- ✓ Annotations to enrich the data models with additional (domain specific) metadata
- ✓ Associations on a conceptual level, replacing joins with simple path expressions in queries
- ✓ Expressions used for calculations and queries in the data model

CDS entities and their metadata are extensible and optimally integrated into the ABAP Data Dictionary and the ABAP language.

CDS is supported natively in both the ABAP and the HANA Platforms! In fact, CDS is the most ambitious and exciting SAP development in the area of data modeling in recent years. You can finally define and consume your data models in the same way (syntax, behaviour, etc.) regardless of the SAP technology platform (ABAP or HANA). Unwantedly the phrase: "One Data Model to rule them all" always comes to mind when I think of CDS.

CDS Support in SAP NW ABAP 7.4 SP5

With SAP NW ABAP 7.4 SP5 the first instalment of CDS support in ABAP has been delivered. This provides you with advanced viewbuilding features which you can use to optimize your data models.

Prerequisite is the ABAP Development Tools for Eclipse (ADT) 2.19 since the new CDS tooling is only available in ABAP in Eclipse.

Create a new DDL source file

You can create a new DDL source in ABAP in Eclipse via *File > New > Other … > ABAP > DDL Source*

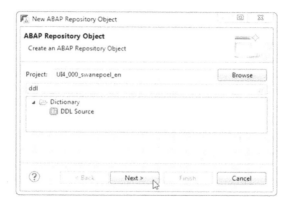

View definition

Your new DDL source is opened in a text editor in ABAP in Eclipse. Initially the source is empty. Using the DEFINE VIEW statement you can define your CDS view entity.

```
3
4   define view SalesOrder as select from snwd_so {
5
6      key so_id as id, //Key field with alias
7
8      billing_status,
9
10     currency_code,
11     gross_amount
12
13  }
14
```

View entities are defined as selects from one or more datasources. Datasources can be other view entities, database tables or classical DDIC views (SE11 views). The select list is defined in curly brackets after the from clause (great for code completion!). The elements in the select list are separated by a comma. The code snippet above defines a simple view entity called SalesOrder on the database table SNWD_SO. SNWD_SO contains the sales orders data.

Currently you can only define one CDS entity per DDL source.

Joining data sources

You can combine records from two or more data sources using join clauses. You can also specify aliases for the datasources.

```
3
4   define view UnpaidSalesOrder as select from snwd_so as so
5   inner join snwd_bpa as bpa on so.buyer_guid = bpa.node_key {
6
7      key so.so_id as id,
8
9      bpa.bp_id as business_partner_id,
10     bpa.company_name,
11
12     'unpaid' as billing_status, //Literal support
13
14     so.currency_code,
15     so.gross_amount
16
17  } where so.billing_status = ' ' //Unpaid
18
```

In addition to INNER JOIN you can also model a LEFT OUTER JOIN, RIGHT OUTER JOIN, UNION and/or UNION ALL.

The comparison operators BETWEEN, =, <>, <, >, <=, >=, NOT and LIKE can be used in the on and where clauses. In addition IS NULL and IS NOT NULL are also valid where-conditions.

Aggregations and SQL functions

CDS also provides support for aggregations (SUM, MIN, MAX, AVG, COUNT), SQL functions (LPAD, SUBSTRING, MOD, CEIL, CAST) and CASE statements in view entities.

```
 5
 6   define view OutstandingSalesOrdersEurope as select from snwd_so as so
 7   inner join snwd_bpa as bpa on so.buyer_guid = bpa.node_key {
 8
 9     bpa.bp_id as business_partner_id,
10
11     substring( bpa.company_name,  0, 10 ) as short_company_name,
12
13     case bpa.bp_role
14       when '01' then 'Customer'
15       when '02' then 'Supplier'
16       else 'Undefined'
17     end as business_partner_role,
18
19     so.currency_code,
20     sum(so.gross_amount) as sum_gross_amount
21
22   }
23   where so.currency_code = 'EUR' and so.billing_status = ' '  //Unpaid
24   group by bpa.bp_id, bpa.company_name, bpa.bp_role, so.currency_code
25   having sum(so.gross_amount) > 100000 //Outstanding amounts > EUR 100.000
26
```

In the above example the view selects the business partners with outstanding sales orders which together (SUM) amount to more than EUR 100.000 (HAVING SUM). The outstanding amounts are reported per business partner role (GROUP BY). The codes for the business partner roles are translated to readable text in the database (CASE).

Semantically rich data models

Annotations can be used to add metadata to CDS entities. Annotations specify the properties and semantics of the entity and its behaviour when it is accessed at runtime. This metadata can also be accessed by consumption tools using special APIs. In future, consumers will be able to extend existing view definitions and add their own annotations without having to re-model the data (*"One Data Model to rule them all"*). Annotations always begin with the @ character.

```
3
4   @AbapCatalog.sqlViewName:  'SALES_ORDER_VW'
5   @AbapCatalog.buffering.status:  #ACTIVE
6   @AbapCatalog.buffering.type:    #SINGLE
7   define view SalesOrder as select from snwd_so {
8
9     key so_id as id,
10
11    billing_status,
12
13    @Semantics.currencyCode currency_code,
14    @Semantics.amount.currencyCode: 'currency_code' gross_amount
15
16  }
17
```

Above the SAP buffering behaviour is specified by using the @AbapCatalog. buffering annotation. Here single record buffering is enabled (prerequisite is that the underlying datasource allows buffering). In addition the element currency_ code is defined as a currency key. The element gross_amount is defined as a currency field and the currency key currency_code is assigned to the field.

In every view definition the **compulsory annotation @AbapCatalog.sqlViewName must be specified**. This annotation specifies the name of the corresponding view in the ABAP Dictionary. CDS entities are integrated into the ABAP Dictionary and ABAP language using the same infrastructure which exists for classical Dictionary views. The CDS entity name (here SalesOrder) can be thought of as an alias for the Dictionary View. The metadata which is specified for the CDS entity, however, can only be accessed via the entity name.

Extensibility

The ABAP Dictionary enhancement concept is also supported in ABAP CDS entites. By using $EXTENSION.* in the select list, all fields that are added as enhancements to the underlying database table or classical DDIC view are automatically added to the CDS entity.

```
 3
 4   @AbapCatalog.sqlViewName: 'SALES_ORDER_VW'
 5   define view SalesOrder as select from snwd_so {
 6
 7     key so_id as id,
 8
 9     billing_status,
10
11     currency_code,
12     gross_amount,
13
14     $extension.*
15
16   }
17
```

Here any fields which are added to the database table SNWD_SO via enhancements, will automatically be added to the view entity. Currently it is only possible to use $EXTENSION.* in view definitions with exactly one datasource (no joins, unions, etc.).

In future, CDS will also provide additional features for extending existing CDS entities themselves (not via the underlying datasource). These features will be available on both the ABAP and HANA platforms.

Consuming your CDS entities in ABAP

Once you have saved and activated your DDL source, the DDIC artifacts are created. Consuming your CDS entity is simple: CDS entities can be used in OPEN SQL! You should always use the entity name in your OPEN SQL statements.

SELECT * FROM SalesOrder INTO TABLE @itab. "Use entity name

Note that when selecting from CDS entities in OPEN SQL, the new OPEN SQL syntax must be used. This means that the ABAP variables (in this case itab) must be escaped using the @ character. The @ character in OPEN SQL has nothing to do with CDS annotations.

Lifecycle and database support

The best part about DDL sources and CDS entities is that they are managed by ABAP. This means that the entire lifecyle of the CDS entities are controlled by the ABAP Change and Transport System (CTS).

In addition, the SP5 CDS features are "open". This means that your CDS view definitions can be deployed on any database which is supported by SAP.

6.4.1.4 SELECTING from TRANSPARENT and POOL TABLES

When selecting from a Transparent or Pool Table, always qualify the SELECT statement as fully as possible with the WHERE option. This includes data fields that may not be part of the key. This allows the database to evaluate the records and return only the records matching the selection criteria.

Example:

* More efficient for Transparent & Pool tables
| ```
SELECT * FROM ZZLT2
   WHERE      RLDNR = V_LDGR
   AND        RRCTY = '0'
   AND        RVERS = '001'
   AND        RYEAR = V_YR
   AND        BUKRS = V_CMPNY
   AND        RACCT = V_ACCT
   AND        RCNTR = V_CNTR.
   .......
ENDSELECT
``` |
| **Will work, but requires more memory & buffers** |
| ```
SELECT * FROM ZZLT2
   WHERE      RLDNR = V_LDGR
   AND        RRCTY = '0'
   AND        RVERS = '001'
   AND        RYEAR = V_YR.
      CHECK V_CMPNY.
      CHECK V_ACCT.
      CHECK V_CNTR.
   .........
ENDSELECT.
``` |

6.4.1.5 SELECTING from CLUSTER TABLES

When working with Cluster tables, only qualify the SELECT statements with fields that are part of the key. If the table is a cluster table, use the CHECK command to eliminate records after the selection has been narrowed via the WHERE clause for key fields.

Cluster tables cannot be processed by the database directly, compared to transparent tables. In most cases forcing the database to unpack and check fields (as with SELECT statements containing non-key fields in WHERE clauses) is less efficient then qualifying only with key fields and letting ABAP check non-key fields after the data is returned.

Example:

For cluster table BSEG with keys MANDT, BUKRS, BELNR, GJAHR, and BUZEI:

* Use the Check statement to evaluate non key fields when selecting from Cluster tables

SELECT * FROM BSEG
WHERE BUKRS = BSIK-BUKRS
AND REBZG = BSIK-BELNR.
  CHECK BSIK-LIFNR = BSEG-LIFNR.
  CHECK BSEG-SHKZG = 'S'.
  CHECK BSEG-KOART = 'K'.
  ....
ENDSELECT.
*Works more efficiently for cluster tables, especially in multiple application server environments.

* With Cluster tables don't specify non-key fields in the WHERE clause
SELECT * FROM BSEG WHERE BELNR = BSIK-BELNR AND BUKRS = BSIK-BUKRS AND LIFNR = BSIK-LIFNR AND SHKZG = 'S' AND KOART = 'K'.   .... ENDSELECT. *Will work, but requires a lot of available memory, buffer space and database time to unpack non-keyed data for verification/inclusion. This work takes place at the database level and can be costly. Can overload single DB servers and slow performance for all user.

6.4.1.6 SELECT Aggregates

When you need to find the maximum, minimum, sum, and average value or the count of a database column, use a select list with aggregate functions instead of computing the aggregates yourself. The network load is considerably less.

Example:

Select using an aggregate function

SELECT MAX(MSGNR) FROM T100 INTO C4A
  WHERE SPRSL = 'D'
  AND ARBGB = '00'.
<div align="center">*More Efficient</div>

Select.... Where + Check

C4A = '000'.
SELECT * FROM T100
  WHERE SPRSL = 'D'.
    CHECK T100-MSGNR > C4A.
    C4A = T100-MSGNR.
ENDSELECT.
<div align="center">*Will work, but not Optimally</div>

6.4.1.7 SELECT with BUFFER support.

Selecting from buffered tables is intended for tables that are frequently used and read-only. Adding the BYPASSING BUFFER parameter to the SELECT statement is less efficient.

Example:

Select without buffer support

SELECT * FROM T100 BYPASSING BUFFER
  WHERE SPRSL = 'D'
    AND   ARBGB = '00'
 	
    AND   MSGNR = '999'.
 	
<div align="center">*4,395 microsec</div>

Select with buffer support

SELECT * FROM T100
  WHERE SPRSL = 'D'
    AND   ARBGB = '00'
    AND   MSGNR = '999'.
<div align="center">*242 microsec</div>

6.4.1.8 Group Level Data Access

In general, external table I/O (table reads, inserts, updates) are much more efficient when done at a group level. Group-level table accesses are less expensive in terms of disk I/O and CPU cycles, and they are usually cleaner and easier to read.

Example 1:

Select into Table
REFRESH I_T006.
SELECT * FROM T006 INTO TABLE I_T006.
*Faster
Select and the append statement
REFRESH I_T006.
SELECT * FROM T006 INTO I_T006.
APPEND I_T006.
ENDSELECT.
*Will work, but if possible, use INTO TABLE

Example 2:

The group update will find all matching rows in the external table and update them with the rows in the internal table.

Group Update using Table
UPDATE TADIR USING TABLE I_OBJECTS.
* More Efficient
Non-group update
LOOP AT I_OBJECTS.
SELECT * FROM TADIR
WHERE PGMID = I_OBJECTS-PGMID
AND   OBJECT = I_OBJECTS-OBJECT
AND   OJB_NAME = I_OBJECTS-OBJ_NAME.
TADIR = INT_OBJECTS.
UPDATE TADIR.
ENDSELECT.
ENDLOOP.
* Less Efficient

6.4.1.9 Column Update

When possible, use column updates instead of single-row updates to update database tables

Example:

Column update
UPDATE VERI_CLNT **SET FUNCTINT = FUNCTINT + 1** * More Efficient
Single line update
SELECT * FROM VERI_CLNT. **VERI_CLNT-FUNCTINT = VERI_CLNT-FUNCTINT + 1.** **UPDATE VERI_CLNT.** **ENDSELECT.** * Will work, but Less Efficient

6.4.1.10 Filling Internal Tables

It is always faster to use the INTO TABLE version of a SELECT statement than to use APPEND statements

Example 1:

Select Into Table
SELECT * FROM T006 **INTO TABLE I_T006.** * More Efficient
Select + Append Statement
REFRESH X006. **SELECT * FROM T006 INTO I_T006.** **APPEND I_T006.** **ENDSELECT.** * Less Efficient

As a general rule, use database views or the INTO TABLE version of a SELECT statement with the addition FOR ALL ENTRIES IN TABLE rather than using nested SELECT statements. The latter is less efficient than using database views but is more efficient than nested selects.

6.4.1.11 Up To nn Rows

The ABAP "UP TO nn" construct causes as many FETCHs to be executed until sufficient rows have been returned to satisfy the nn requirement. When coding a construct of this type, use SQL Trace to examine the output to see how many records can be retrieved with a single FETCH and adjust your OCCURS and UP TO values appropriately. When examining the trace screen, look for the "FETCH xx Array: nnn" statement. This gives the optimum value for the size of the UP TO and OCCURS in the program

6.4.1.12 Explicit Cursor Management

Explicit Cursor Management is a function of SAP Open SQL and consists of three commands:

OPEN CURSOR

FETCH NEXT CURSOR

CLOSE CURSOR

Explicit Cursor Management should be used when it is necessary to traverse a database table with two cursors at the same time.

The following is a simple example showing the use of one cursor:

```
TABLES: RSEUMOD.
 DATA: CURSOR_ONE TYPE CURSOR,
       WA LIKE RSEUMOD.
 OPEN CURSOR CURSOR_ONE FOR
 SELECT * FROM RSEUMOD.
 DO.
 FETCH NEXT CURSOR CURSOR_ONE INTO WA.
 IF SY-SUBRC NE 0.
       CLOSE CURSOR CURSOR_ONE.
       EXIT.
 ENDIF.
 WRITE: / WA-UNAME, WA-DEVCLASS.
 ENDDO.
```

6.5   Implement ABAP Report on HANA Using Native SQL & ADBC

SQL Features

SQL is a largely standardized language for accessing relational databases. It can be divided into three areas -

Data Manipulation Language (DML) – Statements for reading, changing data in database. Example – SELECT, INSERT, UPDATE etc.

Data Definition Language (DDL) – Statements for creating and administrating tables. Example – CREATE TABLE, DROP TABLE etc.

Data Control Language (DCL) – Statements for authorization & consistency checks. Example – GRANT SELECT ON <..> TO <...> etc.

Open SQL

Open SQL consists of a set of ABAP statements that perform operations on the central database in the R/3 System. The results of the operations and any error messages are independent of the database system in use.

Open SQL Features

*   Open SQL provides a uniform syntax and semantics for all of the database systems supported by SAP

*   ABAP Programs that only use Open SQL statements will work in any SAP system, regardless of the database system in use

*   Open SQL statements can only work database tables that have been created in the ABAP Dictionary

*   Open SQL can be used via secondary database connections

Relation of Open SQL to the DML/DDL/DCL aspects of SQL

*   Open SQL Covers the DML aspects (Select, Insert, Update etc.)

*   The ABAP Dictionary tool controls the DDL aspects

*   The DCL aspects are not reflected in standard ABAP;

*   Instead the data access is managed by the ABAP authorization concept.

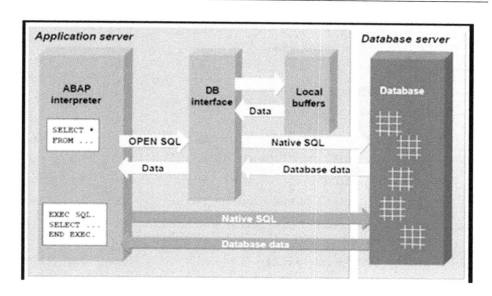

Limitations of Open SQL

- Following features cannot be found in Open SQL
    - Fixed values in field list
    - Computed columns
    - Sub-queries in SELECT or FROM clauses
    - RIGHT OUTER JOIN, FULL JOIN, UNION

Some HANA specific DML are also not covered by Open SQL.

Case Construct in calculated columns

SAP HANA built in functions e.g. – DAYS_BETWEEN( )...

No direct access to SAP HANA views and database procedures

Native SQL

- Native SQL allows us to use database-specific SQL statements in an ABAP program.
- The database tables which are not declared in ABAP dictionary can also be accessed through Native SQL.

- No Syntax check of the SQL statement will be performed
- Use EXEC statement to call Native SQL

  EXEC SQL.
    <Native SQL statement>
  ENDEXEC.

- In Native SQL statements, the data is transported between the database table and the ABAP program using host variables

  e.g –   EXEC **SQL.**
            SELECT connid, cityfrom, cityto
            INTO :wa
          FROM spfli
          WHERE carrid = :c1
          ENDEXEC.

- Sy-subrc will be set to 0 if at least one row is fetched and sy-dbcnt will be the number of rows returned.

ABAP Database Connectivity (ADBC)

- ADBC is an object based API
- It allows native SQL access providing –
  - Flexibility
  - Where used list
  - Error Handling

- Main Classes are –
  - CL_SQL_CONNECTION
  - CL_SQL_STATEMENT
  - CL_SQL_RESULT_SET

- Steps

- Choose database connection
- cl_sql_connection=>get_connection
  - Instantiate the statement object
  - Construct the SQL (check with SQL Console for syntax)
  - Issue Native SQL Call
  - Assign target variable for result set
  - Retrieve Result set
  - Close the query and release resources

ABAP Database Connectivity (ADBC) – Key Points

- No syntax check for native SQL statements
  - Make sure to handle exception cx_sql_exception
- No hashed or sorted tables allowed as target
  - Use standard table
- No automatic client handling
  - Specify MANDT in where condition
- No guaranteed release of allocated resources on DB
  - Close the query

6.6   Full Text Search & ALV on HANA

6.6.1   Using SAP HANA Full Text Search)

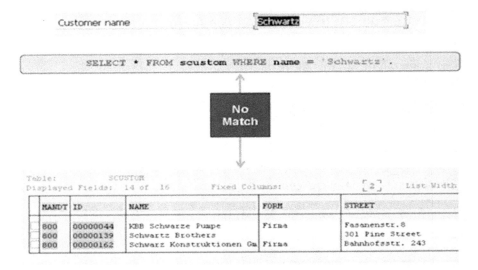

Fuzzy Search – Sometimes Equals Is Not Enough

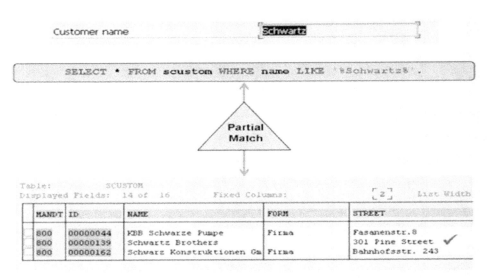

Fuzzy Search – Sometimes LIKE Is Not Enough

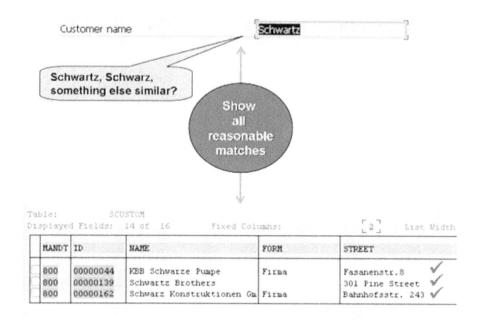

Fuzzy Search – An Error-Tolerant Search

Full text search requires full text indexes

* To get all search features
* For good performance

Column-Store Table must be basis

* Data type TEXT or SHORTTEXT
  → Full text index created automatically

* Data type NVARCHAR
  → Create index using ABAP Dictionary
  (in ABAP 7.4 system)

Remember the memory overhead of the index

Prerequisites For Fuzzy Search

Creating a Full-Text Index for Fuzzy Search

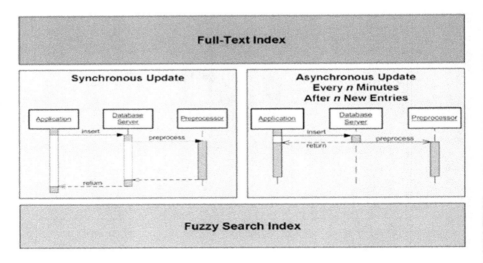

Creating the Index

Creating the index in an ABAP 7.4 system

Example – Table ZCOMPANIES

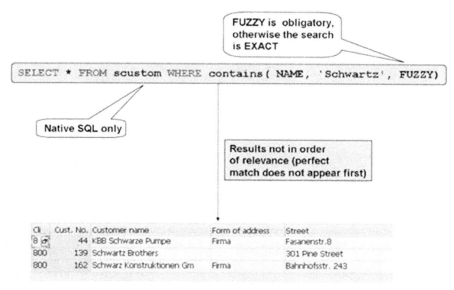

The CONTAINS() Function

- Selection from ABAP program only works for Native SQL
- Example program Z_TEST_FUZZY

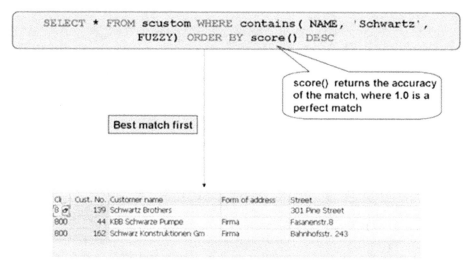

The SCORE() Function

Linguistic Search

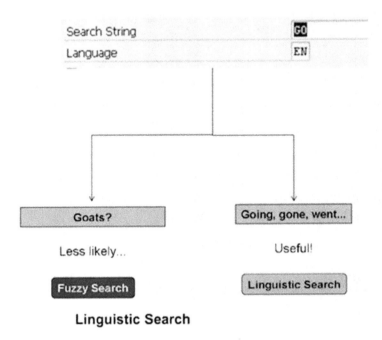

Linguistic Search

Creating a Full-Text Index for Linguistic Search

MANDT	KEY	SPRAS	TEXT	SPRAS_ISO
800	00001	E	He is going	EN
800	00001	D	Er geht	DE
800	00002	E	He went	EN
800	00002	D	Er ging	DE

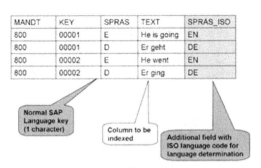

Configuring the Linguistic Search

- From single-character language code, convert to 2-character ISO code using Function Module CONVERT_SAP_LANG_TO_ISO_LANG

> ### LINGANALYSIS_BASIC
>
> Separation of a string into words

> ### LINGANALYSIS_STEMS
>
> Separation of a string into words and identification of
> the root word – GO from *WENT* (EN) or *GEHEN* from *GING* (DE)

> ### LINGANALYSIS_FULL
>
> Separation and stemming as above, but additionally
> tagging of the parts of speech (verb, noun, and so on)

Text Analysis Options

Using the Linguistic Search

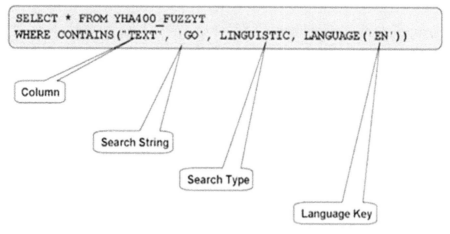

Using the Linguistic Search

Using Full Text Search And Type-Ahead Input Fields

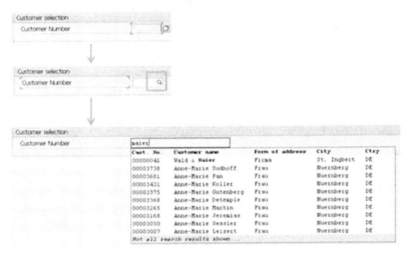

Search Helps with Type-Ahead and Fuzzy Search

Example
- Search Help Z_HANA_SH
- Transaction code Z_TEST_TH

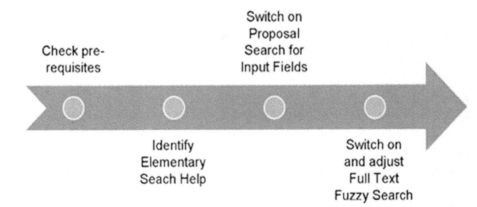

Also enable type-ahead in screen in ABAP 7.4 ≤ SP05

Enabling Type-Ahead With Fuzzy Search for SAP GUI

6.6.2   SAP List Viewer with Integrated Data Access (ALV with IDA)

Basic Principles and Advantages

- **Basic Principles**

  Only retrieve from the database data which is to be displayed on the screen

  Use database services where possible – ALV features pushed down to the database

  Data described declaratively instead of passing big internal tables

- **Advantages**

  Retrieval of results is much faster

  Better performance and reduced memory consumption

  Improved user experience

What is SALV IDA – SAP ABAP List Viewer – Integrated Data Access

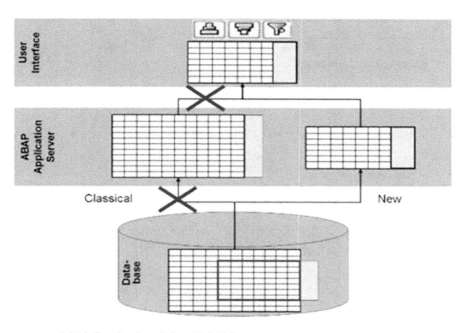

ALV Optimized for HANA

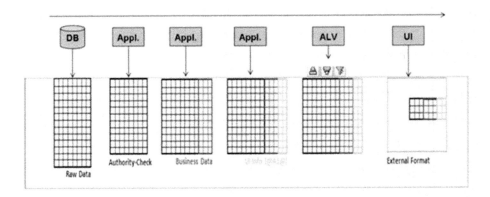

- Relevant data is extracted into an internal table after the application performs the necessary authorization checks
- Calculated Business Data columns may be added by the application
- UI information (for example icons or links) is added
- ALV services manipulate the data (sent via an internal table) based on user interaction
- Required data is displayed on the screen

Classical ALV – How Does it Work

- **Classical ALV Problems**

    Working with huge amounts of data (potentially millions of records)

    Initial Load – All data needs to be loaded from the database into an internal table

    Sorting, filtering, grouping can take a substantial amount of time

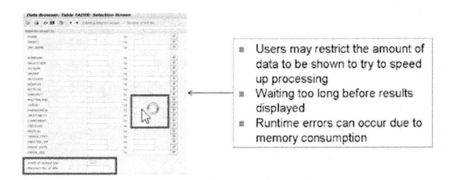

- Users may restrict the amount of data to be shown to try to speed up processing
- Waiting too long before results displayed
- Runtime errors can occur due to memory consumption

Classical ALV – Problems

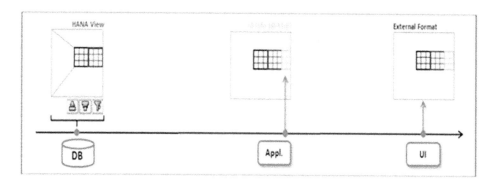

- Authority checks, table functions, paging, sorting, filtering are now performed by the database via the relevant parameters
- UI information is still handled by the application
- Amount of data is severely restricted by the database before it is displayed on the UI and it is not required to store it in an internal table.

The New Approach – ALV Optimized for HANA

Package SALV_IDA_TEST contains sample programs

- Reduced toolbar compared to the classic ALV
- Users can select a column or a cell and make use of several options in the context menus
- The layout, sort and filter settings can also be changed using the Change Layout button

ALV for HANA – End User Perspective

Feature	Classic ALV	ALV for HANA	Limitations for ALV on HANA
Multi-db support	Yes	Not at present	
Sorting	Yes	Yes	Without currency/unit consideration (must first sort on currency/UOM)
Selection Screen	Dealt with by application	Yes – select-options and parameters to be passed to the ALV API	
Filtering	Yes	Yes	
Aggregation	Yes	Yes	No unit/currency split if aggregating amounts/currency values
Grouping	No	Yes	
Find	Yes	No	
Text and Fuzzy Search	No	Yes	
Support for HANA Views	Dealt with by application	Yes	
Authorization Checks	Dealt with by application	Yes	
Export to Excel	Yes	Yes	Restricted to 10,000 records
Printing	Yes	Yes	Restricted to 10,000 records

Availability of Features in ALV for HANA I

Feature	Classic ALV	ALV for HANA	Limitations for ALV on HANA
Personalization	Yes	Yes	
Cells with links, buttons, icons	Yes	No	
Graphics	Yes	No	
Editable	Yes	No	
Fixed Columns	Yes	No	
Double-click	Yes	No	

Availability of Features in ALV for HANA II

Reference variables required for container and also the ALV instance

```
DATA: lo_cont    TYPE REF TO cl_gui_custom_container,
      lo_salv    TYPE REF TO if_salv_gui_table_ida.
```

Create container instance

```
CREATE OBJECT lo_cont
  EXPORTING
    repid          = sy-repid
    dynnr          = '0100'
    container_name = 'ALV_AREA'
  EXCEPTIONS
    OTHERS         = 1.
  IF sy-subrc <> 0.
    MESSAGE a010(yha400).
  ENDIF.
```

Either a database table OR an External View published to the ABAP Dictionary OR a CDS View can be passed to the CREATE method

```
lo_salv = cl_salv_gui_table_ida=>create(
    io_gui_container  = lo_cont
    iv_table_name     = 'SCUSTOM' ).
```

Coding Example – Instantiation of ALV Optimized for HANA

For large amounts of data it is important that a user has the option to restrict the amount of data that is displayed using a selection screen.

```
DATA: lo_range_collector TYPE REF TO cl_salv_range_tab_collector,
      lt_named_ranges     TYPE if_salv_service_types=>yt_named_ranges.

SELECT-OPTIONS:
    so_id FOR gs_scustom-id,
    so_name FOR gs_scustom-name.

* Create ALV Instance

  lo_salv = cl_salv_gui_table_ida=>create(
      io_gui_container  = lo_cont
      iv_table_name     = 'SCUSTOM' ).

* Transform Ranges to one Range Table

  CREATE OBJECT lo_range_collector.

  lo_range_collector->add_ranges_for_name( iv_name  = 'ID'
                                           it_ranges = so_id[] ).

  lo_range_collector->add_ranges_for_name( iv_name  = 'NAME'
                                           it_ranges = so_name[] ).

  lo_range_collector->get_collected_ranges( IMPORTING
                              et_named_ranges = lt_named_ranges ).

* Set Select Options

  lo_salv->set_select_options( EXPORTING
                               it_ranges   = lt_named_ranges ).
```

Restricting Data Display

```
DATA: lo_cont TYPE REF TO cl_gui_custom_container,
      lo_salv TYPE REF TO if_salv_gui_table_ida,
      lo_fcat  TYPE REF TO if_salv_gui_field_catalog_ida,
      lo_exc   TYPE REF TO cx_salv_ida_contract_violation.

* Create Container

CREATE OBJECT lo_cont
  EXPORTING
    repid          = sy-repid
    dynnr          = '0100'
    container_name = 'ALV_AREA'
  EXCEPTIONS
    OTHERS         = 1.
IF sy-subrc <> 0.
  MESSAGE a010(yha400).
ENDIF.

* Create ALV Instance

lo_salv = cl_salv_gui_table_ida->create(
    io_gui_container    = lo_cont
    iv_table_name       = 'YHA400_CUSTWDAYS' ).

* Set Data Elements for columns

TRY.
    lo_fcat = lo_salv->field_catalog( ).

    lo_fcat->set_data_element( iv_field_name       = 'ID'
                               iv_data_element_name = 'S_CUSTOMER' ).

  CATCH cx_salv_ida_contract_violation INTO lo_exc.
    MESSAGE lo_exc TYPE 'I'.
ENDTRY.
```

Referencing Data Elements for ALV Columns

```
* References for container and ALV
DATA: lo_cont TYPE REF TO cl_gui_custom_container,
      lo_salv TYPE REF TO if_salv_gui_table_ida,
      lt_params TYPE if_salv_gui_types_ida->yt_parameter,
      ls_params LIKE LINE OF lt_params.

* Create Container

CREATE OBJECT lo_cont
  EXPORTING
    repid          = sy-repid
    dynnr          = '0100'
    container_name = 'ALV_AREA'
  EXCEPTIONS
    OTHERS         = 1.
IF sy-subrc <> 0.
  MESSAGE a010(yha400).
ENDIF.

* Create ALV Instance

lo_salv = cl_salv_gui_table_ida->create(
    io_gui_container    = lo_cont
    iv_table_name       = 'YHA400_CUSTWDAYS' ).  "External view with input parameter

* Set Parameter
ls_param-name = 'FLIGHTS_BEFORE'.
ls_param-value = sy-datum.

APPEND ls_param TO lt_params.
lo_salv->set_view_parameters( lt_params ).
```

Method SET_VIEW_PARAMETERS must be called to supply values for any
input parameters if an External View is the data source

ALV Using External View with Parameters

```
DATA lo_alv_display TYPE REF TO if_salv_gui_table_ida.
DATA lo_container_d0555 TYPE REF TO cl_gui_custom_container.
PARAMETERS p_sterm TYPE string VISIBLE LENGTH 18.
PARAMETERS p_simil TYPE p LENGTH 2 DECIMALS 1.

    CREATE OBJECT lo_container_d0555
      EXPORTING
        CONTAINER_NAME = 'D0555_CONTAINER'
      EXCEPTIONS
        others         = 6.

    IF SY-SUBRC <> 0.
      MESSAGE 'Could not create container' TYPE 'E'.
    ENDIF.

    lo_alv_display = cl_salv_gui_table_ida=>create( iv_table_name   = 'SFLIGHT'
                                                     io_gui_container = lo_container_d0555 ).

    lo_alv_display->text_search( )->set_field_similarity( p_simil ).
    lo_alv_display->text_search( )->set_search_term( p_sterm ).

    call screen 0555.
```

Fuzzy Search Functionality with ALV for HANA

- The **Data Display** is restricted to a maximum of 2 billion **cells**. All available operations are then executed on the entire data amount even if this exceeds the maximum display size.
- **If an External View is the data source**
- Use field catalog object to reference suitable data element for each column, column headings will be derived from this data element
- Don't forget to supply suitable values for any input parameters

ALV for HANA: Things to Keep in Mind

Summary: Code-to-Data Techniques

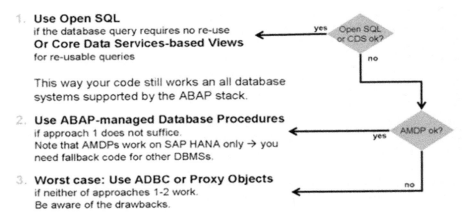

1. **Use Open SQL**
   if the database query requires no re-use
   Or Core Data Services-based Views
   for re-usable queries

   This way your code still works an all database
   systems supported by the ABAP stack.

2. **Use ABAP-managed Database Procedures**
   if approach 1 does not suffice.
   Note that AMDPs work on SAP HANA only → you
   need fallback code for other DBMSs.

3. **Worst case: Use ADBC or Proxy Objects**
   if neither of approaches 1-2 work.
   Be aware of the drawbacks.

Summary: Which Code-to-Data Technique to Use?

The implementation of in-memory databases can lead to significant technical changes in many areas with the processing of large quantities of data; users profit from the required data being displayed more quickly, and from the additional funcions. To make the great advantages usable for business applications in the ALV environment as well, SAP offers a special version of the List Viewer, the SAP List Viewer with Integrated Data Access. Using ALV with IDA it is possible for tables that contain very large quantities of data to be displayed on the UI. The results of operations such as sorting, grouping, or filtering are also delivered with a very fast response time.

Advantages

The SAP List Viewer with Integrated Data Access offers application developers the option to use the in-memory database, such as SAP HANA, without having to switch to a new programming environment. End users can continue to work on the familiar interface. The standard functions (also ALV services) that have been used in the ALV for a long time for executing calculations are still available in ALV with IDA. From the perspective of a user, the whole ALV with its well-known ALV functions is adjusted to the use of in-memory databases. The new general programming model (CodingPushDown) is also optimally supported when using in-memory databases.

6.7   String Manipulation

6.7.1   Concatenate

Use the CONCATENATE statement instead of programming a string concatenation.

Example:

Use of the CONCATENATE statement

MOVE 'Jane'   TO V_MA.
MOVE 'Miller' TO V_MB.
MOVE 'New York City' TO V_MC.
CONCATENATE 'Mrs.'
        V_MA V_MB
        'from'
        V_MC INTO CHA SEPARATED BY SPACE.
 	
"Mrs. Jane Miller from New York City" is the final value of CHA
 	
* More Efficient

Moving with Offset
MOVE 'Jane'   TO V_MA. MOVE 'Miller' TO V_MC. I1 = STRLEN(V_MA). I2 = STRLEN(V_MB) MOVE 'Mrs.' TO V_CHA. MOVE V_MA   TO CHA+5. I1 = I1 + 6. MOVE V_MB   TO CHA+11. 1 = I1 + I2 + 1. MOVE 'from 'TO CHA+I1.I1 = I1 + 5. MOVE V_MC   TO CHA+11. "Mrs. Jane Miller from New York City" is the final value of CHA * Less Efficient

Some string manipulation functions have become obsolete in Release 3.0 and can be replaced by an ABAP/4 statement or functions:

STRING_CONCATENATE	→CONCATENATE	STRING_SPLIT
→SPLIT	STRING_LENGTH	→STRLEN()
STRING_CENTERED	→WRITE ... TO ... CENTERED	STRING_MOVE_RIGHT
→*WRITE ... TO ... RIGHT-JUSTIFIED		

Example:

Use of the CONCATENATE Statement

CONCATENATE T100-ARGGB
    T100-MSGNR
    T100-TEXT   INTO V_CLA.
 	
        * Standard in Release 3.0

Use of a CONCATENATE function module

CALL FUNCTION 'STRING_CONCATENATE_3'
  EXPORTING
    STRING1 = T100-ARGGB
    STRING2 = T100-MSGNR
    STRING3 = T100-TEXT
  IMPORTING
    STRING = V_CLA
  EXCEPTIONS
    TOO_SMALL = 01.
 	
       * Obsolete in Release 3.0

6.7.2 Removing Leading Spaces

If leading spaces in a string are to be deleted, use the ABAP/4 statement

SHIFT ... LEFT   DELETING LEADING

Avoid using SHIFT inside a WHILE loop.

Example:

Using SHIFT ... LEFT DELETING LEADING
" V_CLA contains the sting " '   Editor line n'. SHIFT V_CLA LEFT DELETING LEADING SPACE.   * More Efficient

Shifting by SY-FDPOS places
" V_CLA contains the sting " '   Editor line n'. IF V_CLA CN SPACE. ENDIF. SHIFT V_CLA BY SY-FDPOS PLACES LEFT. <div align="center">* Less Efficient</div>

6.7.3   Split

Use the SPLIT statement instead of programming a string split.

Example:

Use of the SPLIT statement

* V_CMA contains '(410)-45174-66354312' and shall be * split into V_AREA_CD, V_TEL_NBR1, TEL_NBR2
 	
SPLIT V_CMA AT '-' INTO V_AREA_CODE
          V_TEL_NBR1
          V_TEL_NBR2.
 	
<div align="center">* More Efficient</div>

Use of SEARCH and MOVE with offset
V_CMA contains '(410)-45174-66354312' and shall be * split into AREA_CD, TEL_NBR1, TEL_NBR2. SEARCH V_CMA FOR '-'. MOVE V_CMA(SY-FDPOS) TO V_AREA_CD. I1 = SY-FDPOS + 2. SEARCH V_CMA FOR '-' STARTING AT I1. I1 = I1 - 1. MOVE V_CMA+I1(SY-FDPOS) TO TEL_NBR1. I1 = I1 + SY-FDPOS + 1. MOVE V_CMA+I1 TO TEL_NBR2. <div align="center">* Less Efficient</div>

6.7.4 Strlen()

Use STRLEN() function to restrict the DO loop to relevant part of the field, e.g. when determining a CHECK_SUM.

Example:

Get a CHECK_SUM with strlen( )
| ```
DATA: BEGIN OF  STR,
       LINE TYPE X,
       END OF STR,
       CHECK_SUM  TYPE I.

"MOVE 'KALEBVPQDSCFG' TO CLA.

I1 = STRLEN( CLA ).
DO I1 TIMES VARYING STR FROM CLA NEXT CLA+1.
    CHECK STR NE SPACE.
    ADD STR-LINE TO CHECK_SUM.
ENDDO.
``` |
| * More Flexible |
| **Get a CHECK_SUM with field length** |
| ```
DATA: BEGIN OF STR,
       LINE TYPE X,
        END OF STR,
       CHECK_SUM  TYPE I.

MOVE 'KALEBVPQDSCFG' TO CLA.

DO 64 TIMES VARYING STR FROM CLA NEXT CLA+1.
    CHECK STR NE SPACE.
    ADD STR-LINE TO CHECK_SUM.
ENDDO.
``` |
| * More Flexible |

To find out the length of a field use the string length function.

Example:

* More Efficient
FLDLEN = STRLEN (FLD).
* Less Efficient
IF FLD CP '* #'. **ENDIF.** **FLDLEN = SY-FDPOS.**

6.8   Field-Symbols

Use the ASSIGN and FIELD-SYMBOLS statements to provide the powerful functionality of pointers. FIELD-SYMBOLS are place holders for fields. A FIELD-SYMBOL does not occupy memory, but points to a position that has been ASSIGNed to the FIELD-SYMBOL at runtime. After the FIELD-SYMBOL has been ASSIGNed to an object, it can be worked with the same way as the object itself.

Example:

A data string contains two types of fields. Field 1 contains the length of Field 2; Field 3 contains the length of Field 4. This occurs until the length field contains 0 or the total length is over 3000.

```
PARAMETERS:                                    P_FL_IN(70).

DATA:                                 INPT_RCRD(3000),
                    POSITION     TYPE I,
        LENGTH      TYPE N.                        FIELD-
SYMBOLS <ENTRY>.

DO.                                              READ
DATASET P_FL_IN   INTO   INPT_RCRD.       IF SY-SUBRC NE
0.                              EXIT.
                  ENDIF.
        LENGTH = INPT_RCRD+POSITION(3).                IF
LENGTH = 0.                           EXIT.
                  ENDIF.
              ADD 3 TO POSITION.
        ASSIGN INPT_RCRD+POSITION(LENGTH) TO <ENTRY>.
   WRITE <ENTRY>.                               IF
POSITION >= 3000.                      EXIT.
                  ENDIF.
              ENDDO.
```

Considerations:

- As FIELD-SYMBOL references are only established at runtime, the syntax does not always detect errors such as type conflicts. This could cause runtime errors or incorrect data assignments. As of Release 3.0, to avoid the possibility of a type conflict, you can declare FIELD-SYMBOLS with a TYPE.

6.9   General Statements

- Logical expressions are evaluated from left to right. The evaluation is ended when the final result has been established (elimination or complete inclusion). Therefore, when using AND or OR operator (in IF, WHERE, etc.), the most likely elimination criterion should be specified first. The opposite will be true for negative comparisons and some OR conditions.

Example:

The following table is to be read with printing of employees from ABC company in Georgia:

EMPLOYEE	NAME	COMPANY	STATE
001	Doe, J	ABC	TX
002	Doe, M	ABC	OK
003	Jones, A.	XYZ	TX
004	Jones, B.	ABC	GA
005	Jones, C.	ABC	TX
006	Jones, D.	XYZ	GA
007	Jones, E.	ABC	TX
008	Smith, A.	ABC	GA
009	Smith, B.	ABC	TX
010	Smith, C.	ABC	OK

Less Efficient
IF COMPANY = 'ABC'   **AND STATE = 'GA'.**   **WRITE ...**   **ENDIF.**   Will work, but will need to evaluate both the company and state fields for eight of ten records.

More Efficient
IF STATE = 'GA'   **AND COMPANY = 'ABC'.**   **WRITE ...**   **ENDIF.**   Will need more time to process, since it can eliminate all records without STATE = 'GA' and therefore will need to evaluate both company and state for only 3 records.

• Use special operators CO (Contains Only), CA (Contains Any), CS (Contains String) instead of programming the operations yourself. If ABAPs statements are executed per character on long strings, CPU consumption can rise substantially.

Example:

Do-Loop with Field-Symbols

ASSIGN CHA(1) TO <C>.
 DO 200 TIMES.
  IF <C> = '(' OR <C> = ')'.
   "..... any actions
   EXIT.
  ENDIF.
  ASSIGN <C>+1 TO <C>.
 ENDDO.
 	
                                          1263 microsec

Using the CA Operator

IF CHA(200) CA '()'.
  "... any actions.
 ENDIF.
                                          443 microsec

- When testing fields "equal to" something, use either the nested IF or the CASE statement. The CASE is better for two reasons. It is easier to read and after about five nested IFs the performance of the CASE is more efficient.

- When records a and b have the exact same structure, it is more efficient to MOVE a to b than to MOVE-CORRESPONDING a to b, if records a and b have the exact same structure.

Example:

More Efficient
MOVE BSEG TO *BSEG
Less Efficient
MOVE-CORRESPONDING BSEG TO *BSEG

6.10 Logging On to HANA system

6.11 Connect to SAP HANA database from HANA Studio

Step 1: Open HANA Studio. Right-click in the Navigator window and select "Add System".

Step 2: Specify Hostname, Instance Number and Description. Press Next.

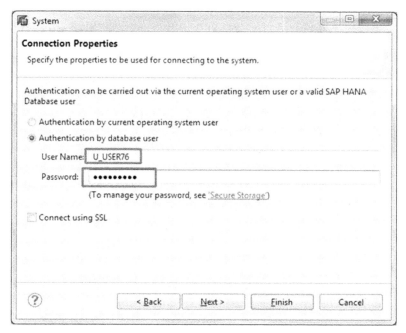

Step 3: Specify Username and Password. Click Next.

Step 4: Click Finish.

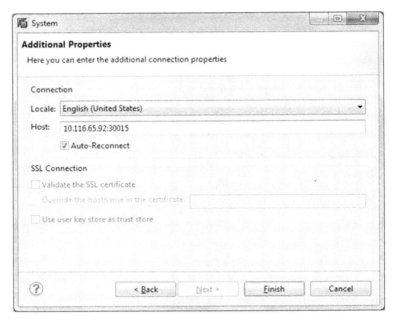

Connect to SAP HANA database from Eclipse

Step 1: Open the Eclipse tool. Ensure that you are in the SAP HANA Modeler perspective (if not already) by following the menu-path *Window Open Perspective SAP HANA Modeler*

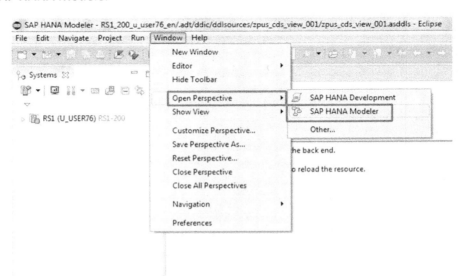

Step 2: Right-click in the Systems window and select "Add System".

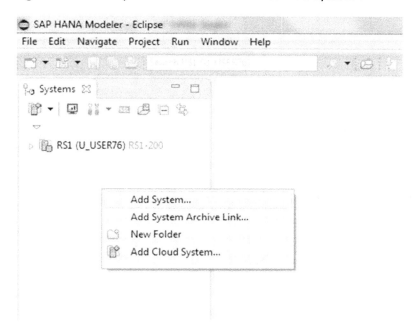

Step 3: Specify Hostname, Instance Number and Description. Press Next.

Step 4: Specify Username and Password. Click Next.

Step 5: Press Finish.

Connect to SAP ABAP terminal from Eclipse

Step 1: Open the Eclipse tool. Ensure that you are in the SAP HANA Development perspective (if not already) by following the menu-path *Window Open Perspective SAP HANA Development*

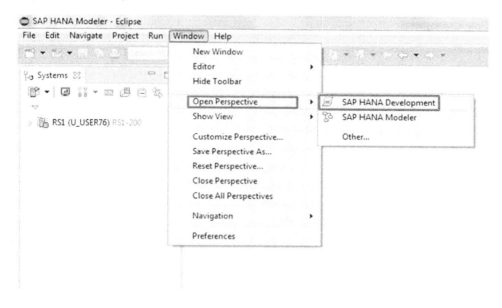

Step 2: Right-click in the Project Explorer Workspace and select **New Project ABAP → ABAP Project.**

Press Next.

Step 3: Select Radio button "Select Connection from SAP Logon" and press Browse.

Step 4: Select the System you want to create the connection for and press OK.

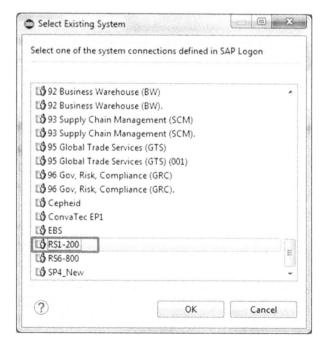

Step 5: The Connection parameters gets filled automatically. Press Next.

Step 6: Specify Client, Username and Password. Press Next.

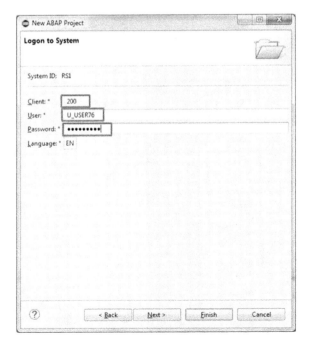

Step 7: Press Finish.

2. Creating Package (for HANA Data Modeling)

Step 1: Ensure that you are in the SAP HANA Modeler perspective in ADT (or HANA Studio). The screenshots shown below are from ADT.

Step 2: In the Systems window, expand the HANA Database system for which you want to create the Package. Right-click on the Content folder and follow the menu-path *New Package*.

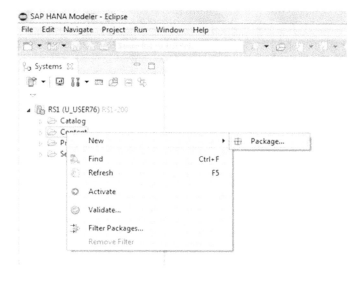

Step 3: Enter Name and Description. Press OK.

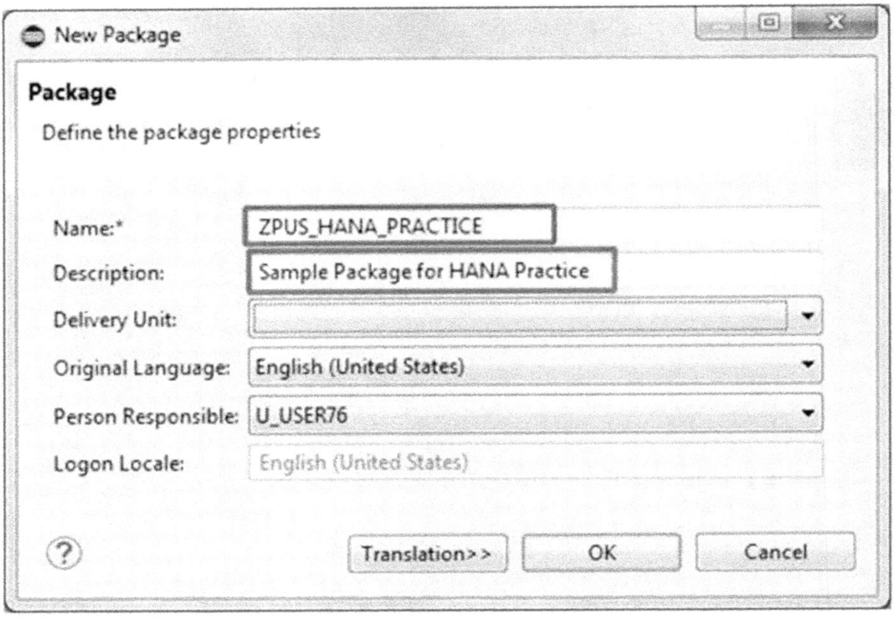

3. Creating HANA Views

All the 3 views (i.e. Attribute, Analytic and Calculation) should be created from the SAP HANA Modeler perspective in ADT (or HANA Studio). The screenshots shown below are from ADT.

Attribute Views

In the following steps, we will create an Attribute View by joining 2 tables SCUSTOM (Customer) and SBOOK (Flight Bookings). This view will also include one calculated Column that will contain how many days ahead each Booking was made (i.e. Days between The Order Date and Flight Date).

Step 1: Under Content folder, right-click on the Package and follow menu-path *New Attribute View...*

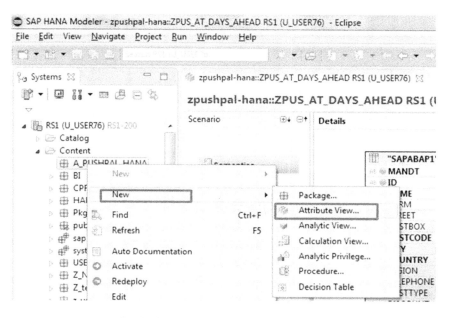

Step 2: Enter Name and Label. Click Finish

Step 3: Select "Data Foundation" in the Scenario window and press "Add Objects" button.

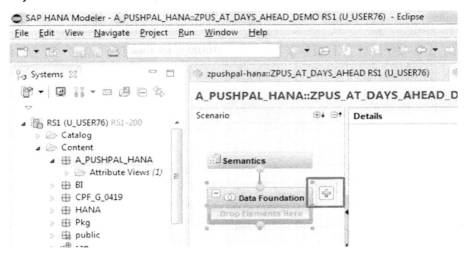

Step 4: Type the name of the Table in the search box. A list of Matching Items will be shown. Select the correct Table and press OK.

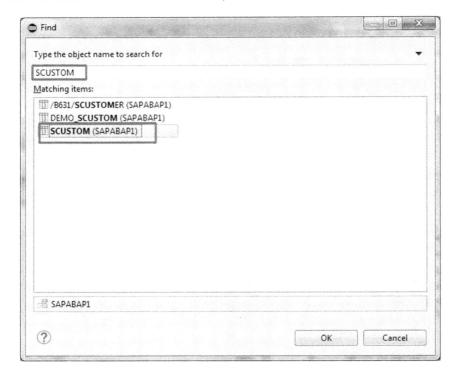

Step 5: Repeat Step 4 to add another Table SBOOK. The following will be the result.

Step 6: Join the relevant fields in the 2 tables, by dragging from a field in SCUSTOM to the corresponding join field in SBOOK. For each joined field, check the Join Type and Cardinality and adjust if necessary

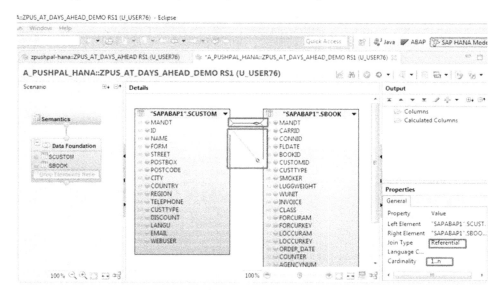

Step 7: In both the tables, add fields to the View output by clicking on the grey round buttons preceding each fieldname. An Orange button indicates that this field has been added to the Output.

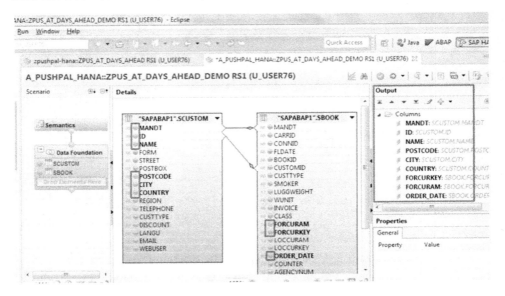

Step 8: Apply a Filter (hard-coded) on specific Fields. In this case, we will exclude all Cancelled Bookings, and will apply a filter on SBOOK.CANCELLED <> 'X'. For this, right-click on the field, and select "Apply Filter…"

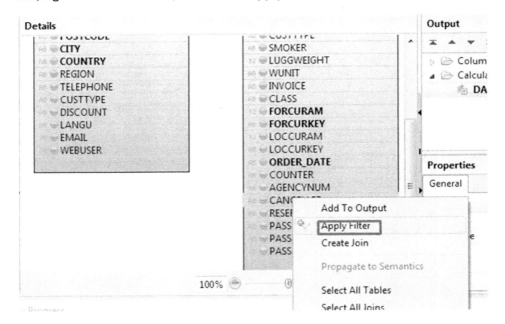

Enter the Filter-criteria as follows and press OK.

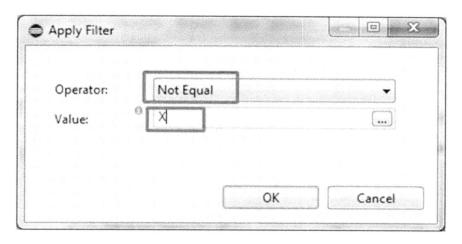

Step 9: Add a Calculated field "DAYS_AHEAD" by right-clicking on "Calculated Columns" and selecting "New...".

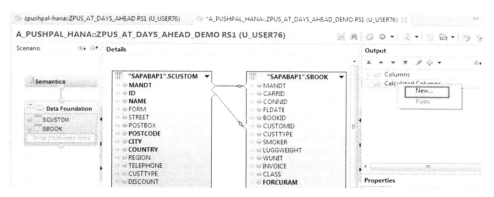

In the subsequent screen, enter the Name, Label, Data-type, Length (if applicable) and the Expression.

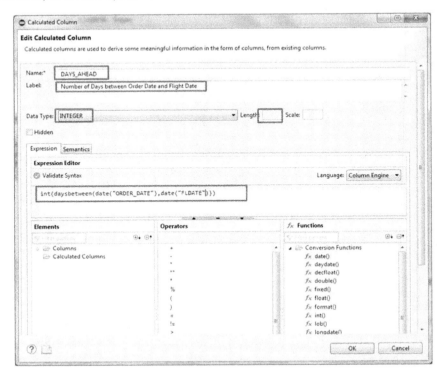

In the Semantics tab, specify an appropriate Semantic Type (if applicable). In this case, we will not select anything.

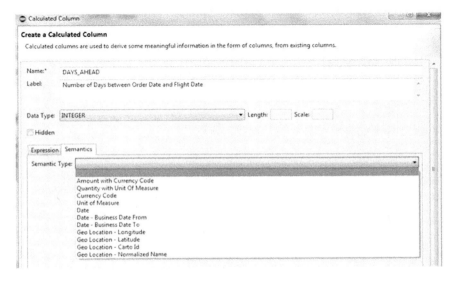

Press OK.

Step 10: Select "Semantics" (in Scenario window) and set each view column properties (Key fields, Semantic Type, Label Column and Hidden). *An Attribute View MUST have Key fields defined.*

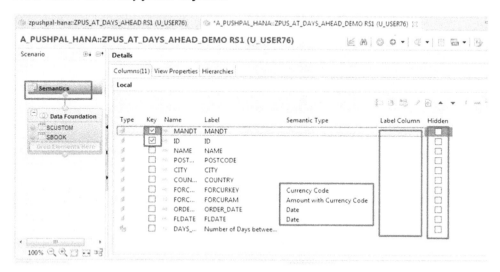

In the "View Properties" tab, select the Default Client.

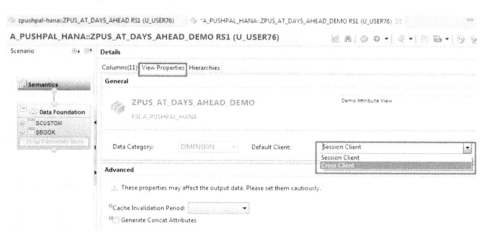

Step 11: Press "Save and Validate Changes to this Object". If no errors are encountered, then press "Save and Activate".

Step 12: Press the "Data Preview" button to display the View data in a new Window.

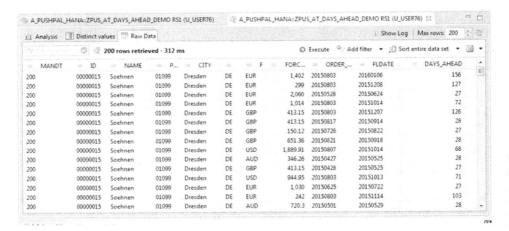

4. <u>Analytic Views</u>

In the following steps, we will create an Analytic View by joining 2 tables SCUSTOM (Customer) and SBOOK (Flight Bookings). This view will also include one calculated Column that will convert the Booking Amount in Foreign Currency to "USD".

Step 1: Under "Content" folder, right-click on your Package and select *New Analytic View*

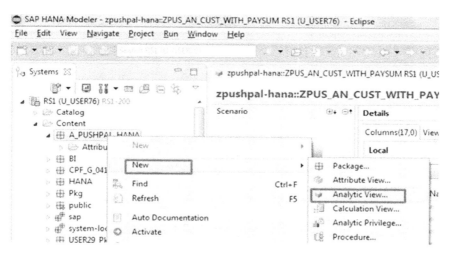

Step 2: Enter Name and Label. Click Finish.

Step 3: As demonstrated in Attribute Views, add the table SCUSTOM and SBOOK to the Data Foundation. Then join the tables (with correct Join Type and Cardinality). Select the Output fields. Apply Filter on CANCELLED column.

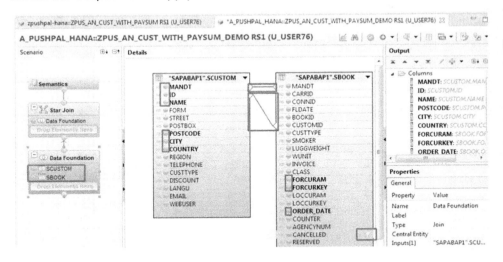

Step 4: Add a new Calculated Column "PAYSUM_CONV" (that will convert the Booking Amount in Foreign Currency to USD). For this, first select "Star Join" window. Then Right-click on "Calculated Columns" (under Output window) and select "New Calculated Column..."

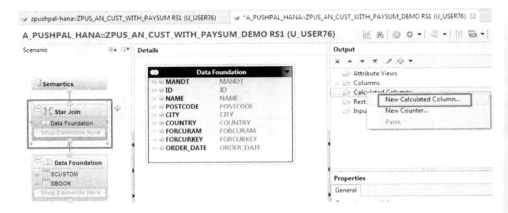

Enter all the values as highlighted in red in the screen below.

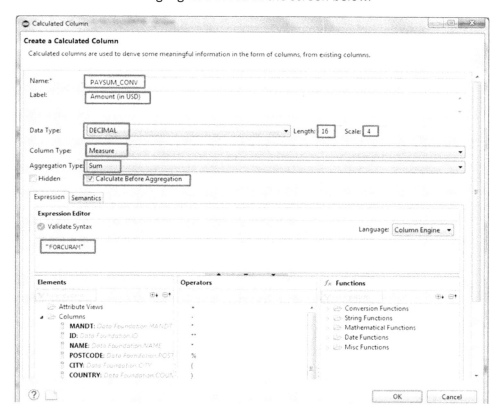

In the "Semantics" tab, enter the Currency conversion details (as highlighted in red in the screen below).

Press OK.

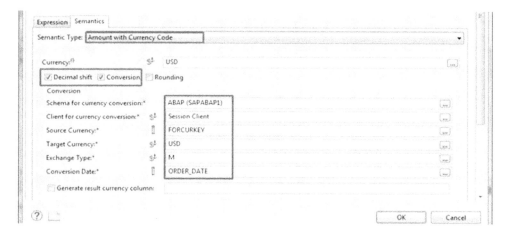

Step 5: Select "Semantics" scenario, and mark the column-type as "Attributes" or "Measure" for all the columns. For Analytic views, at least one column must be a Measure. Also, define the Semantic Type for the columns.

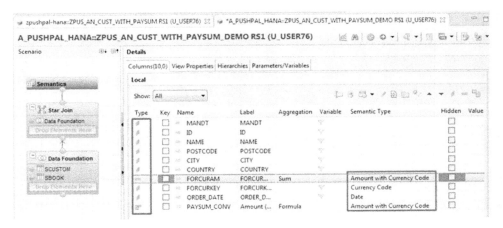

Step 6: Press "Save and Validate Changes to this Object". If no errors are encountered, then press "Save and Activate". Display the data by pressing "Data Preview".

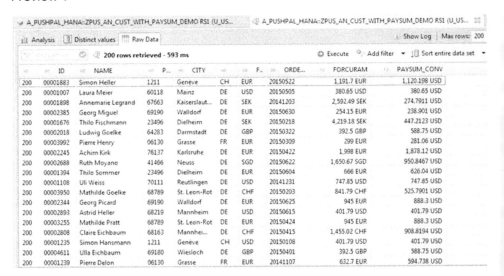

5. Calculation Views

In the following steps, we will create a Calculation View (using the Scripting method) by using the Attribute View created above. This view will also include one calculated Column that will contain for each Customer the average days ahead each Booking was made (i.e. Days between The Order Date and Flight Date).

Step 1: In the "Content" folder, right-click on your Package and select *New Calculation View...*

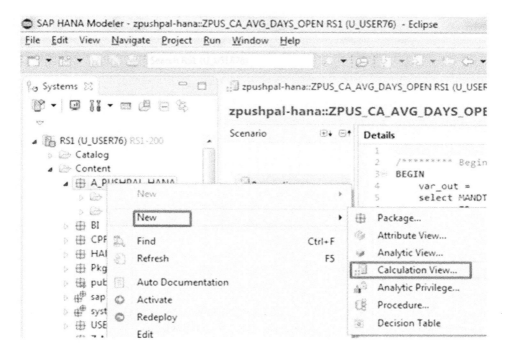

Step 2: Enter the Name, Label, Type and Parameter Case Sensitive details as shown in the screen below.

Press Finish.

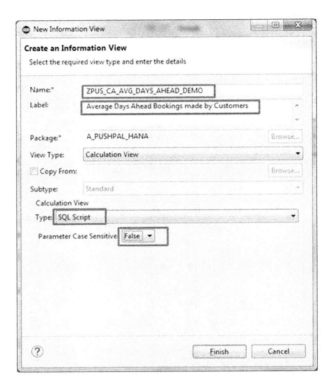

Step 3: Select "Script_View" and first, manually add the Output Columns by selecting New Add Columns From... (in Output window)

Select the Attribute View created above and press Next.

Select the list of fields to be copied from output of Attribute View to the Calculation View and press Finish.

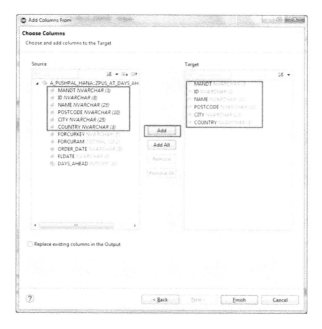

Step 4: Next, add a calculated column "AVG_DAYS_AHEAD" by right-clicking on "Columns" and selecting "Edit Columns"

Enter the details of the new calculated Column (i.e. Name, Data Type, Length and Scale). Press OK.

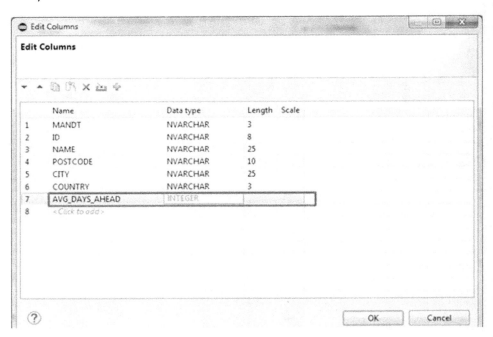

Step 5: Add an Input Parameter "FLIGHTS_BEFORE" by selecting New New Input Parameter... (in Output window)

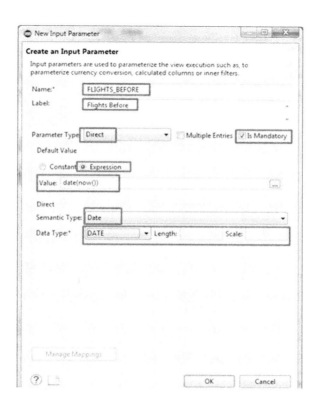

Step 6: Copy-paste the below SQL procedure script in the Details window, to retrieve/calculate the view fields:

/********* Begin Procedure Script ************/

BEGIN

var_out =

    select   mandt, id, name, postcode, city, country,

            avg(days_ahead) as avg_days_ahead

     from   "A_PUSHPAL_HANA::ZPUS_AT_DAYS_AHEAD_DEMO"

    where fldate < :flights_before

    group by mandt, id, name, postcode, city, country;

END /********* End Procedure Script ************/

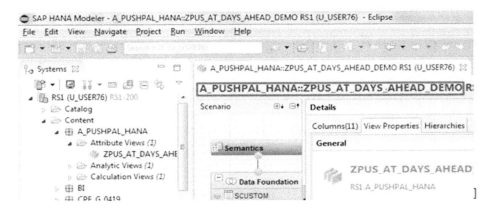

[HINT: In order to know how to specify the full-path of Attribute View in the FROM clause below, open the Attribute View from the Content folder. The full path will be as shown in the title bar (as highlighted below):

Step 7: Select the "Semantics" scenario and ensure that the Column Type, Semnatic Type and Client-handling has been maintained correctly.

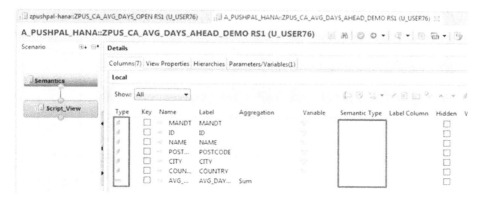

Step 8: Press "Save and Validate Changes to this Object". If no errors are encountered, then press "Save and Activate". Display the data by pressing "Data Preview". Since this View has an Input parameter, the following window is displayed. Modify the value of "FLIGHTS_BEFORE" and press OK.

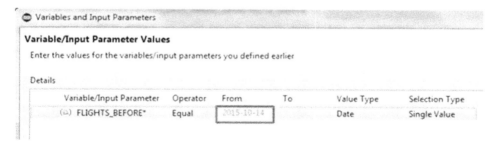

The following Output is displayed.

MANDT	ID	NAME	POSTCODE	CITY	COUNTRY	AVG_DAYS_AHEAD
200	00000015	Soehnen	01099	Dresden	DE	29
200	00000005	Martin	L07 1AZ	Liverpool	GB	17
200	00000010	Raupp	8002	Zuerich	CH	23
200	00000004	Staerck	69115	Heidelberg	DE	16
200	00000008	Moore	SW3 4DE	London	GB	22
200	00000013	Mueller	68159	Mannheim	DE	29
200	00000025	SAP Australi...	NSW 2060	Sydney	AU	39
200	00000016	Leihinger Br...	80339	Muenchen	DE	28
200	00000017	Ruthenberg	69118	Heidelberg	DE	30
200	00000022	SAP (Schwei...	2500	Biel	CH	36
200	00000007	King	M21 7AB	Manchester	GB	20
200	00000011	Ballmann	69115	Heidelberg	DE	22
200	00000012	Radetzky	1000	Wien	AT	23

6. Creating Stored Procedures

In this section, we will create a Stored Procedure that will retrieve the first N and last N Customers from the Attribute View created above, based on their Average Days Ahead Bookings. The value of N will be determined by an Input Parameter IM_NUMBER. Also, the client will be determined by another Input Parameter IM_ CLIENT. This Procedure will return 2 result-sets having the same structure.

Step 1: Ensure that you are in the SAP HANA Modeler perspective (if not already). In the Content folder, right-click on your Package and select New Procedure...

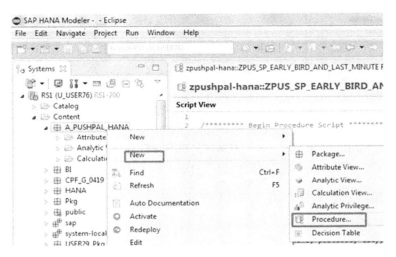

Step 2: Enter the Name, Label, Default Schema and Run With details and press Finish.

Step 3: First, add 2 Input Parameters "IM_CLIENT" and "IM_NUMBER" by right-clicking on "Input Parameters" (in Input Pane window) and selecting "New Scalar Parameter…"

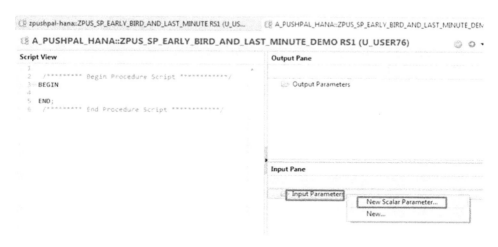

Enter the Name, Data Type, Length and Scale and press OK.

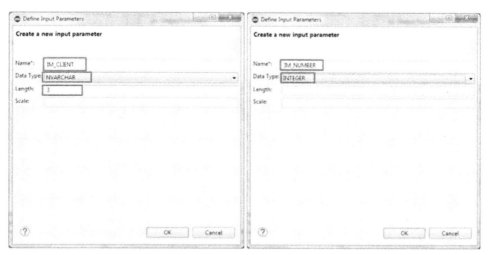

Step 4: Next, add 2 Output Parameters "ET_EARLY" and "ET_LATE" by right-clicking on "Output Parameters" (in Output Pane window) and selecting "New…"

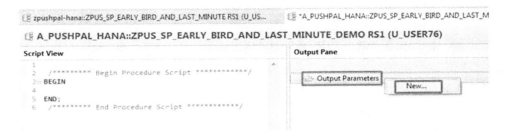

Create the 2 Output Parameters by filling the Structure Names and the fields. In this case, both ET_EARLY and ET_LATE has the same structure.

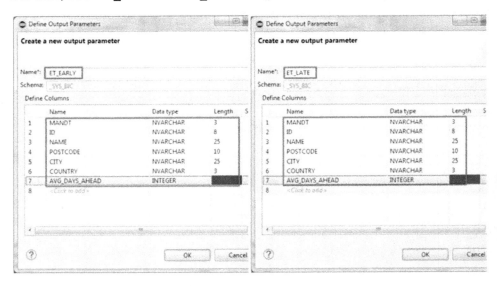

Step 5: Copy-paste the below SQL Script Procedure in the Script View window to populate the Output Parameters.

/********* Begin Procedure Script ************/

BEGIN

et_early =

  select top :im_number

            mandt, id, name, postcode, city, country,

            avg(days_ahead) as avg_days_ahead

    from "_SYS_BIC"."A_PUSHPAL_HANA/ZPUS_AT_DAYS_AHEAD_DEMO"

  where mandt = :im_client

  group by mandt, id, name, postcode, city, country

  order by avg(days_ahead) desc;

  et_late =

  select top :im_number

            mandt, id, name, postcode, city, country,

            avg(days_ahead) as avg_days_ahead

    from "_SYS_BIC"."A_PUSHPAL_HANA/ZPUS_AT_DAYS_AHEAD_DEMO"

  where mandt = :im_client

  group by mandt, id, name, postcode, city, country

          order by avg(days_ahead) asc;

END;

/********* End Procedure Script ************/

Step 6: Press "Save and Validate Changes to this Object". If no errors are encountered, then press "Save and Activate". To test the procedure, open a new SQL window by selecting Catalog (in the Systems window), and pressing "Open SQL Console for Selected System".

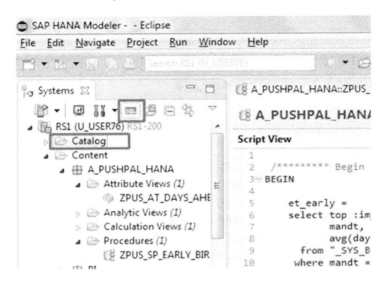

In the SQL Console, enter the following SQL query:

CALL

"_SYS_BIC"."A_PUSHPAL_HANA/ZPUS_SP_EARLY_BIRD_AND_LAST_MINUTE_ DEMO"('200',10,null,null)

The following 2 output windows are displayed, one each for the 2 Output
Parameters ET_EARLY and ET_LATE

*RS1 - SQL Console 1

RS1 (U_USER76) 10.116.65.92 00

SQL   Result   Result
CALL "_SYS_BIC"."A_PUSHPAL_HANA/ZPUS_SP_EARLY_BIRD_AND_LAST_MINUTE_DEMO"('200',10,null,null)

	MANDT	ID	NAME	POSTCODE	CITY	COUNTRY	AVG_DAYS_AHEAD
1	200	00002147	Thilo Jacqmain	23496	Dielheim	DE	191
2	200	00004182	Florian Heller	69180	Wiesloch	DE	181
3	200	00002483	Cindy Kramer	76018	Arlingt…	US	178
4	200	00001581	Fabio Montero	00195	Roma	IT	176
5	200	00003594	Thomas Pratt	60657	Chicago	US	172
6	200	00004179	Amelie Dom…	68753	Amelie	DE	172
7	200	00000674	Astrid Jacqm…	68219	Mannh…	DE	171
8	200	00004511	August Picard	66464	Homb…	DE	170
9	200	00000212	Werk 1200 Dr…	10069	Dresden	DE	169
10	200	00003840	Jean-Luc Illner	75839	Paris	FR	169

*RS1 - SQL Console 1

RS1 (U_USER76) 10.116.65.92 00

SQL   Result   Result
CALL "_SYS_BIC"."A_PUSHPAL_HANA/ZPUS_SP_EARLY_BIRD_AND_LAST_MINUTE_DEMO"('200',10,null,null)

	MANDT	ID	NAME	POSTCODE	CITY	COUNTRY	AVG_DAYS_AHEAD
1	200	00003622	Holm Meier	69121	Heidelberg	DE	14
2	200	00003960	Adam Buchholm	69483	Wald-Michelbach	DE	14
3	200	00003621	Anna Wohl	86343	Koenigsbrunn	DE	15
4	200	00004076	Ruth Neubasler	41466	Neuss	DE	15
5	200	00001472	Lothar Kreiss	69180	Walldorf	DE	15
6	200	00003056	Marta Madeira	08014	Barcelona	ES	16
7	200	00002833	Matthias Martin	69123	Heidelberg	DE	17
8	200	00000005	Martin	L07 1AZ	Liverpool	GB	17
9	200	00004299	Salvador Delon	41006	Sevilla	ES	17
10	200	00001590	Christine Lind…	68163	Mannheim	DE	18

7. Consuming Views and Stored Procedures

The Views (Attribute, Analytic and Calculation) and Stored Procedures created from HANA Data Modeler perspective resides in the HANA database and is not accessible directly from the ABAP layer. Hence we cannot write Open SQL syntax to access these views or procedures. For this, we have to use the ADBC (ABAP DataBase Connectivity)/External Views/Database Procedure Proxy approach, as outlined below.

Consuming HANA Views

There are 2 approaches of consuming HANA Views as outlined below:

Native SQL/ADBC Method (from both ADT and SAP GUI):

The program shown below accesses the Calculation View created above, BUT the approach is absolutely same for accessing Attribute or Analytic views.

The following program takes as input a Date (corresponding to Flights Before) and displays the list of all Average Days Ahead of all Customers who had bookings before the Input Date.

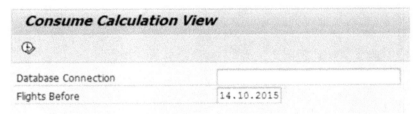

Consume Calculation View

Cust. No.	Customer name	Postal Code	City	Co	
15	Soehnen	01099	Dresden	DE	29
5	Martin	L07 1AZ	Liverpool	GB	17
10	Raupp	8002	Zuerich	CH	23
4	Staerck	69115	Heidelberg	DE	16
8	Moore	SW3 4DE	London	GB	21
13	Mueller	68159	Mannheim	DE	29
25	SAP Australia PTY.LTD.	NSW 2060	Sydney	AU	39
16	Leihinger Brauerei	80339	Muenchen	DE	28
17	Ruthenberg	69118	Heidelberg	DE	30
22	SAP (Schweiz) AG	2500	Biel	CH	36
7	King	M21 7AB	Manchester	GB	20
11	Ballmann	69115	Heidelberg	DE	22
12	Radetzky	1000	Wien	AT	23
19	Plum	69493	Großsachsen	DE	32
3	Hans Bullinger	69119	Heidelberg	DE	16
14	Genee	50733	Koeln	DE	26
21	SAP Oesterreich	1221	Wien	AT	37
2	Andreas Klotz	69190	Walldorf	DE	14
18	Miller	46539	Dinslaken	DE	37
20	Becker	69181	Leimen	DE	33

Creating and Consuming SAP HANA Artifacts and ABAP Artifacts for SAP HANA

The following is the source code of the above program:

REPORT zpus_consumeca_vew.

```
*   Output Data declarations
    TYPES: BEGIN OF gy_customer,
        id TYPE s_customer,
        name    TYPE s_custname,
        postcode        TYPE postcode,
        city    TYPE city,
        country TYPE s_country,
        days_ahead TYPE i,
        END OF gy_customer.

    DATA lt_customers TYPE STANDARD TABLE OF gy_customer.

*   ADBC related declarations
    DATA: lo_connection TYPE REF TO cl_sql_connection,
        lo_sql          TYPE REF TO cl_sql_statement,
        lo_result       TYPE REF    TO cl_sql_result_set,
        lv_sql          TYPE string,
        lr_data         TYPE REF    TO  data.

*   Exception related declarations
    DATA: lx_sql_exception TYPE REF TO cx_sql_exception,
        lv_text   TYPE string.

*   ALV display related declarations DATA: lo_alv TYPE REF TO cl_salv_table,
        lx_msg  TYPE REF TO cx_salv_msg.

*   Selection-Screen Definition PARAMETERS: p_con TYPE dbcon_name,
        p_datum TYPE sydatum.

*   Database Access
    START-OF-SELECTION.

        TRY.
        ·  Get Database Connection
        ·  lo_connection = cl_sql_connection=>get_connection( p_con ).
        ·  Create Instance of SQL CREATE OBJECT lo_sql
        ·  EXPORTING
        ·  con_ref = lo_connection
```

· Build SQL statement

```
lv_sql = | SELECT ID, NAME, POSTCODE, CITY, COUNTRY, AVG_DAYS_AHEAD
| && | FROM  "_SYS_BIC"."A_PUSHPAL_HANA/ZPUS_CA_AVG_DAYS_
AHEAD_DEMO" | && | ('PLACEHOLDER'=('$$flights_before$$', '{ p_datum
}')) | && | WHERE MANDT = { sy-mandt } | .
```

· Execute SQL Query

```
lo_result = lo_sql->execute_query( lv_sql ).
```

· Get Reference of Query Result into Output GET REFERENCE OF lt_
customers INTO lr_data. lo_result->set_param_table(lr_data). lo_
result->next_package( ). lo_result->close( ).

```
CATCH cx_sql_exception INTO lx_sql_exception.
lv_text = lx_sql_exception->get_text( ).
MESSAGE i398(00) WITH lv_text.
LEAVE LIST-PROCESSING.
ENDTRY.
```

· Output Display

```
END-OF-SELECTION.
IF NOT lt_customers IS INITIAL.
```

· Display Output TRY.

```
        cl_salv_table=>factory(
                MPORTING r_salv_table = lo_alv
                CHANGING
                        t_table = lt_customers ).

        lo_alv->display( ).

CATCH cx_salv_msg INTO lx_msg.
        lv_text = lx_msg->get_text( ).
        MESSAGE i398(00) WITH lv_text.
        LEAVE LIST-PROCESSING.
        ENDTRY.
        ENDIF.
```

Creating External Views in ADT (Proxy approach):

In this approach, an External View is created in the ABAP layer, which acts as a proxy for the underlying

HANA View. *Note that this approach cannot be followed if the underlying HANA view has Input Parameters*. Follow the steps shown below:

Step 1: Ensure that you are in the ABAP perspective in ADT. Right-click on your Package and follow the menu-path *New Other ABAP Repository Object Dictionary Dictionary View and press NEXT.*

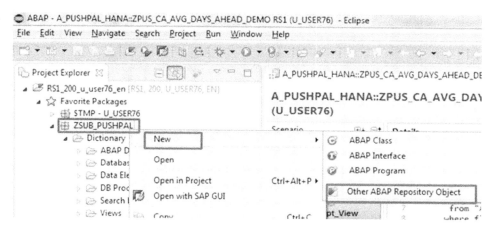

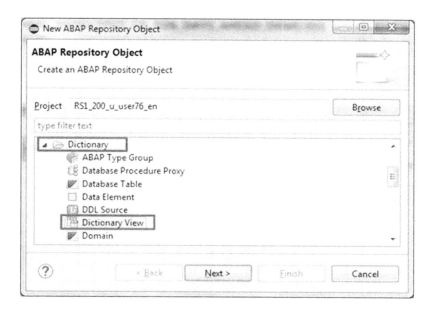

Step 2: Enter the Name and Description. Select the Radio-button for "External View" and then enter the underlying HANA View. Press NEXT.

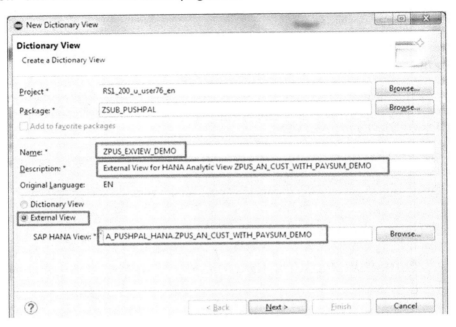

Step 3: Select the TR and press FINISH.

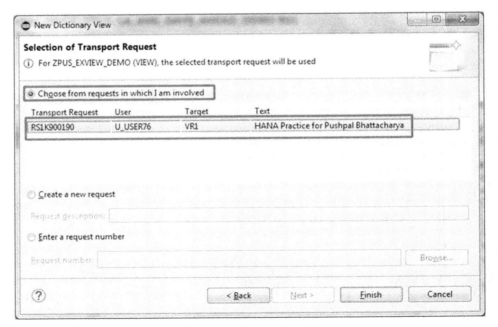

Step 4: Activate the External View. Note the Synchronize Button. This External View must be synchronized when any changes are made to the underlying HANA View.

| @ [RS1] ZPUS_CONSUME_EXT_VIEW | ▾ A_PUSHPAL_HANA::ZPUS_AN_CUST_WITH_PAYSUM_... | [RS1] ZPUS_EXVIEW_DEMO | |

Dictionary View: ZPUS_EXVIEW_DEMO

General Attributes

| View Type: | External View | | | | | Synchronize |
| SAP HANA View: | A_PUSHPAL_HANA.ZPUS_AN_CUST_WITH_PAYSUM_DEMO | | | | | |

Fields

DDIC Name	DDIC Type	Length	Decimals	SAP HANA Name	SAP HANA Type
MANDT	CLNT	3	0	MANDT	NVARCHAR(3)
ID	CHAR	8	0	ID	NVARCHAR(8)
NAME	CHAR	25	0	NAME	NVARCHAR(25)
POSTCODE	CHAR	10	0	POSTCODE	NVARCHAR(10)
CITY	CHAR	25	0	CITY	NVARCHAR(25)
COUNTRY	CHAR	3	0	COUNTRY	NVARCHAR(3)
FORCURKEY	CHAR	5	0	FORCURKEY	NVARCHAR(5)
ORDER_DATE	CHAR	8	0	ORDER_DATE	NVARCHAR(8)
FORCURAM	DEC	15	2	FORCURAM	DECIMAL(15,2)
PAYSUM_CONV	DEC	16	4	PAYSUM_CONV	DECIMAL(16,4)
ROW_COUNT	DEC	18	0	row.count	DECIMAL(18)

Now the above external view can be consumed directly in our ABAP code using Open SQL syntax.

REPORT zpus_consume_ext_view.

START-OF-SELECTION.

SELECT id,
        name,
        postcode,
        city,
        country,
        AVG(paysum_conv) AS usd_amount,
        'USD' AS to_curr

INTO TABLE @DATA(lt_customers)

FROM zpus_exview_demo

GROUP BY id, name, postcode, city, country.

IF sy-subrc = 0.

cl_demo_output=>display_data(value = lt_customers

name   = 'Consuming HANA View through External View').

ENDIF.

🗗 Output

Consuming HANA View through External View

ID	NAME	POSTCODE	CITY	COUNTRY	USD_AMOUNT	TO_CURR
00004067	Anna Martin	86343	Koenigsbrunn	DE	1.20133824E4	USD
00000690	Johann Kramer	11111	Berlin	DE	1.06128356E4	USD
00002422	Christa Columbo	64342	Seeheim-Jugenheim	DE	1.8215126E4	USD
00002591	Simon Fischmann	1211	Genève	CH	1.9193583500000001E4	USD
00003572	Claire Henry	68163	Mannheim-Lindenhof	DE	1.3201363799999999E4	USD
00002502	Matthias Hansmann	69123	Heidelberg	DE	1.6623608400000001E4	USD
00000523	Juan Montero Soria	28017	Madrid	ES	1.49593032E4	USD
00000735	Peter Mechler	16233	Potsdam	DE	9.9126988000000001E3	USD
00003473	Guenther Matthaeus	79104	Freiburg	DE	1.7553570500000002E4	USD
00002490	Ruth Heller	41466	Neuss	DE	1.7214324000000001E4	USD
00000492	Peter Henry	16233	Potsdam	DE	1.8992492900000001E4	USD
00000012	Radetzky	1000	Wien	AT	2.2965682799999999E4	USD
00001734	Astrid Wohl	68219	Mannheim	DE	1.3098513800000001E4	USD
00002553	Stephen Eichbaum	68723	Schwetzingen	DE	1.0850781199999999E4	USD
00000166	Buffetti S.p.A.	20100	Milano	IT	1.9860416700000002E4	USD
00003188	Dominik Dumbach	75305	Neuenburg	DE	2.0044038499999999E4	USD

Consuming Stored Procedures

Accessing Stored Procedures can be in 2 different ways as shown below. The following program takes as input "No. of Customers" and returns 2 grids in the output. The upper grid represents the Top N Customers with Highest Average Days Ahead Booking. Similarly, the bottom grid represents the Top N Customers with Lowest Average Days Ahead Booking.

Native SQL/ADBC Method (from both ADT and SAP GUI)

This approach is absolutely similar to the ADBC approach of Consuming Views.

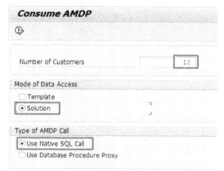

The above Output is the same as that obtained in Section 4 (where we consumed the Stored Procedure through a SQL script).

DB Procedure Proxy Method (from ADT only)

For this, we first need to create a DB Procedure Proxy from ADT by performing the following steps:

Step 1: Ensure that you are in the ABAP perspective (if not already). In Project Explorer, right-click on your ABAP Package, and select New Other ABAP Repository Object Dictionary Database Procedure Proxy. Click Next.

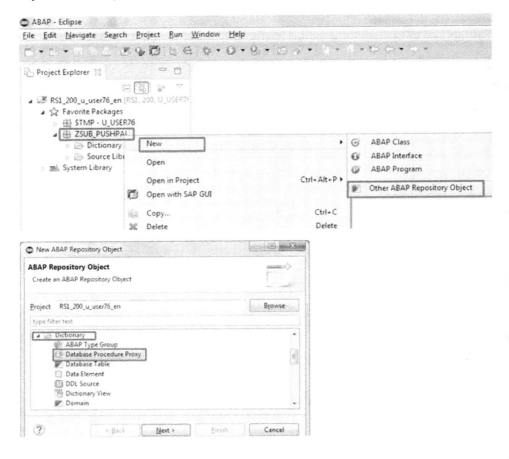

Step 2: Fill in the details shown below and press Next.

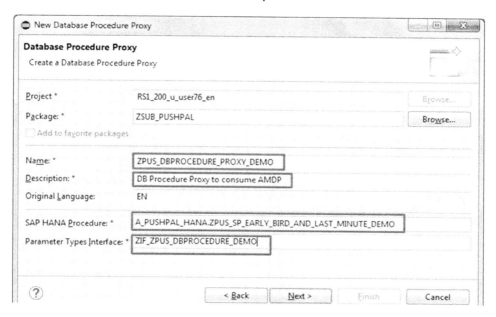

Step 3: Select the Transport details and press Finish.

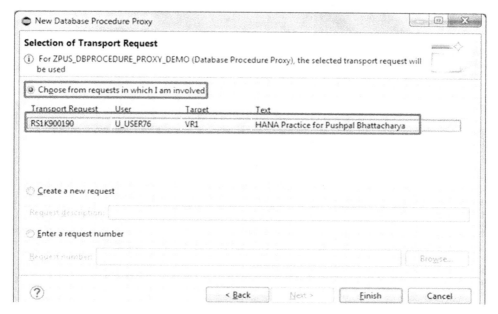

Step 4: In order to ensure that there are no Data-type mismatch when calling this DB Procedure Proxy from ABAP program, override Component Types with ABAP Dictionary Types.

*[RS1] ZPUS_DBPROCEDURE_PROXY_DEMO

Database Procedure Proxy: ZPUS_DBPROCEDURE_PROXY_DEMO

General Attributes

SAP HANA Procedure: A_PUSHPAL_HANA.ZPUS_SP_EARLY_BIRD_AND_LAST_MINUTE_DEMO

Database Procedure Interface: ZIF_ZPUS_DBPROCEDURE_DEMO

Parameters

SAP HANA Name	SAP HANA Type	ABAP Name	ABAP Type	DDIC Type Override
⊃▸ IM_CLIENT	NVARCHAR(3)	IM_CLIENT	C length 3	S_MANDT
⊃▸ IM_NUMBER	INTEGER	IM_NUMBER	I	
▲ ◀⊐ ET_EARLY	A_PUSHPAL_HAN...	ET_EARLY		
MANDT	NVARCHAR(3)	MANDT	C length 3	S_MANDT
ID	NVARCHAR(8)	ID	N length 8	S_CUSTOMER
NAME	NVARCHAR(25)	NAME	C length 25	S_CUSTNAME
POSTCODE	NVARCHAR(10)	POSTCODE	C length 10	POSTCODE
CITY	NVARCHAR(25)	CITY	C length 25	CITY
COUNTRY	NVARCHAR(3)	COUNTRY	C length 3	S_COUNTRY
AVG_DAYS_AHEAD	INTEGER	AVG_DAYS_AHEAD	I	
▲ ◀⊐ ET_LATE	A_PUSHPAL_HAN...	ET_LATE		
MANDT	NVARCHAR(3)	MANDT	C length 3	S_MANDT
ID	NVARCHAR(8)	ID	N length 8	S_CUSTOMER
NAME	NVARCHAR(25)	NAME	C length 25	S_CUSTNAME
POSTCODE	NVARCHAR(10)	POSTCODE	C length 10	POSTCODE
CITY	NVARCHAR(25)	CITY	C length 25	CITY
COUNTRY	NVARCHAR(3)	COUNTRY	C length 3	S_COUNTRY
AVG_DAYS_AHEAD	INTEGER	AVG_DAYS_AHEAD	I	

Step 5: Activate the DB Procedure Proxy. Now this Proxy can be called from inside our ABAP Code as shown below.

The following is the source code of the program:

```
REPORT zpus_consume_sp.
```

- Structure for Result TYPES: BEGIN OF gy_customer,

```
        mandt   TYPE s_mandt,
        id      TYPE s_customer,
        name    TYPE s_custname,
        postcode        TYPE postcode,
        city    TYPE    city,
        country TYPE    s_country,
        avg_days_ahead TYPE i, "ha400_avgnd,
        END OF gy_customer.
```

```
TYPES: gy_t_customers TYPE STANDARD TABLE OF gy_customer.
```

```
*   Data objects
```

```
*   Tables for results
```

```
DATA: gt_cust_early   TYPE gy_t_customers,
        gt_cust_late    TYPE gy_t_customers.
```

```
* Screen processing
DATA: ok_code   TYPE syucomm,
        save_ok_code TYPE syucomm.
```

```
* selection screen
SELECTION-SCREEN BEGIN OF BLOCK    cus WITH FRAME TITLE text-cus.
PARAMETERS: p_num TYPE i DEFAULT 10.
SELECTION-SCREEN END OF BLOCK cus.
SELECTION-SCREEN BEGIN OF BLOCK    b1 WITH FRAME TITLE text-t01.
PARAMETERS: p_temp   TYPE xfeld         RADIOBUTTON GROUP exe DEFAULT 'X',
        p_solu   TYPE xfeld       RADIOBUTTON GROUP exe.
SELECTION-SCREEN END OF BLOCK b1.
SELECTION-SCREEN BEGIN OF BLOCK    b2 WITH FRAME TITLE text-t02.
PARAMETERS: p_native TYPE xfeld         RADIOBUTTON GROUP typ DEFAULT 'X',
        p_proxy         TYPE xfeld       RADIOBUTTON GROUP typ.
SELECTION-SCREEN END OF BLOCK b2.
```

```
START-OF-SELECTION.
        CASE abap_true.
        WHEN p_temp.  " template only
        PERFORM get_data_template    USING  p_num
                        CHANGING gt_cust_early
                              gt_cust_late.
        PERFORM display USING gt_cust_early
              gt_cust_late.
        WHEN p_solu.  " solution only
        PERFORM get_data_solution    USING  p_num
                        CHANGING gt_cust_early
                              gt_cust_late.
        PERFORM display USING gt_cust_early
              gt_cust_late.
        ENDCASE.
*&      ----------------------------------------------------------------      *
*&      Form  get_data_template
*&      ----------------------------------------------------------------      *
FORM get_data_template USING          uv_number TYPE i
                CHANGING       ct_cust_early TYPE gy_t_customers
                        ct_cust_late  TYPE gy_t_customers.


CLEAR: ct_cust_early,
        ct_cust_late.
TRY.

* Create statement object (primary DB connection) DATA(lo_sql) =
        NEW cl_sql_statement( ).

* First query (fill ct_cust_late)
        DATA(lo_result) = lo_sql->execute_query(

        |SELECT TOP { uv_number } | &&
        |       mandt, id, name, postcode, city, country, AVG(days_ahead) AS
        avg_days_ahead | &&
        |       FROM _SYS_BIC."zpushpal-hana/ZPUS_AT_DAYS_AHEAD" | &&
```

```
        | WHERE mandt = { sy-mandt } | &&
        | GROUP BY mandt, id, name, postcode, city, country | &&
        | ORDER BY AVG(days_ahead) ASC |
        ).
lo_result->set_param_table( REF #( ct_cust_late ) ).
lo_result->next_package( ).
lo_result->close( ).
```

- Second query (fill et_cust_early)) lo_result = lo_sql->execute_query(
```
        |SELECT TOP { uv_number } | &&
        |        mandt, id, name, postcode, city, country, AVG(days_ahead) AS
        avg_days_ahead | &&
        |        FROM _SYS_BIC."A_PUSHPAL_HANA/ZPUS_AT_DAYS_AHEAD_
        DEMO" | &&
        | WHERE mandt = { sy-mandt } | &&
        | GROUP BY mandt, id, name, postcode, city, country | &&
        | ORDER BY AVG(days_ahead) DESC |
        ).
lo_result->set_param_table( REF #( ct_cust_early ) ).
lo_result->next_package( ).
lo_result->close( ).
```

```
* Exception handling
        CATCH cx_sql_exception INTO DATA(lo_sql_exc). "Excpt. Class for SQL
        Error
                MESSAGE lo_sql_exc TYPE 'I'.
                LEAVE LIST-PROCESSING.
        ENDTRY.


ENDFORM.        "


*&---------------------------------------------------------------------*
*&      Form    get_data_solution
*&---------------------------------------------------------------------*
FORM get_data_solution USING uv_number TYPE i
CHANGING ct_cust_early TYPE gy_t_customers
```

ct_cust_late   TYPE gy_t_customers.

* Type for result overview TYPES: BEGIN OF ly_overview,
          param TYPE string, value TYPE string,
          END OF ly_overview.

* Data objects for result overview
          DATA lt_overview TYPE STANDARD TABLE OF ly_overview. FIELD-SYMBOLS
          <lfs_overview> TYPE ly_overview.

```
**  ADBC Objects and Variables
*  DATA: lo_con          TYPE REF TO cl_sql_connection,
*  lo_sql                    TYPE REF TO cl_sql_statement,
```
* lo_result   TYPE REF TO cl_sql_result_set,
```
*  lr_data                   TYPE REF TO data.
*
```

* Exception Handling
* DATA lo_sql_exc TYPE REF TO cx_sql_exception.

          CLEAR: ct_cust_early,
          ct_cust_late.

          CASE abap_true.
                  WHEN p_native.
                          TRY.

* Create statement object (primary DB connection)
* CREATE OBJECT lo_sql.

DATA(lo_sql) = NEW cl_sql_statement( ).

* Call Procedure with Overview (fill lt_overview) DATA(lo_result) = lo_sql->execute_query(
                          |CALL
"_SYS_BIC"."A_PUSHPAL_HANA/ZPUS_SP_EARLY_BIRD_AND_LAST_MINUTE_
DEMO"(| &&

|{ sy-mandt }, { uv_number }, null , null) WITH OVERVIEW |).

- GET REFERENCE OF lt_overview INTO lr_data.
- lo_result->set_param_table(lr_data).

   lo_result->set_param_table(REF #(lt_overview)).

   lo_result->next_package( ).

   lo_result->close( ).

- Retrieve first result (Parameter et_early)

   READ TABLE lt_overview ASSIGNING <lfs_overview> WITH KEY param = 'ET_EARLY'.

   lo_result = lo_sql->execute_query(|SELECT * FROM { <lfs_overview>-value } |).

- GET REFERENCE OF ct_cust_early INTO lr_data.
- lo_result->set_param_table(lr_data).

   lo_result->set_param_table(REF #(ct_cust_early)).

   lo_result->next_package( ).

   lo_result->close( ).

- Retrieve second result (Parameter et_late)

   READ TABLE lt_overview ASSIGNING <lfs_overview> WITH KEY param = 'ET_LATE'.

   lo_result = lo_sql->execute_query(|SELECT * FROM { <lfs_overview>-value } |).

- GET REFERENCE OF ct_cust_late INTO lr_data.
- lo_result->set_param_table(lr_data).

   lo_result->set_param_table(REF #(ct_cust_late)).

   lo_result->next_package( ).

   lo_result->close( ).

* Exception handling

   CATCH cx_sql_exception INTO DATA(lo_sql_exc). "Excpt. Class for SQL Error MESSAGE lo_sql_exc TYPE 'I'.

   LEAVE LIST-PROCESSING.

   ENDTRY.

```
            WHEN p_proxy.
                  CALL DATABASE PROCEDURE zpus_dbprocedure_proxy_demo
                        EXPORTING
                              im_client = sy-mandt
                              im_number = uv_number
                        IMPORTING
                              et_early = ct_cust_early
                              et_late  = ct_cust_late.


            ENDCASE.

ENDFORM.         "
*&---------------------------------------------------------------------*
*&      Form      output
*&---------------------------------------------------------------------*
FORM display USING ut_cust_early TYPE gy_t_customers
ut_cust_late       TYPE gy_t_customers.


DATA: lo_cont_1 TYPE REF TO cl_gui_custom_container,
lo_cont_2          TYPE REF TO cl_gui_custom_container,
lo_alv_1           TYPE REF TO cl_salv_table,
lo_alv_2           TYPE REF TO cl_salv_table,
lo_msg TYPE REF TO cx_salv_msg.


• create containers CREATE OBJECT lo_cont_1
            EXPORTING
            container_name = 'UPPER_AREA'
            repid     = sy-repid

dynnr             = '0100'
EXCEPTIONS
OTHERS            = 1.
IF sy-subrc <> 0.
            MESSAGE i398(00) WITH 'Error Creating Container Control'.
            LEAVE LIST-PROCESSING.
ENDIF.
```

```
CREATE OBJECT lo_cont_2
      EXPORTING
            container_name =        'LOWER_AREA'
            repid           =       sy-repid
            dynnr           =       '0100'
      EXCEPTIONS
            OTHERS          =       1.
IF sy-subrc <> 0.
      MESSAGE i398(00) WITH 'Error Creating Container Control'.
      LEAVE LIST-PROCESSING.
      ENDIF.

*   create salv grid controls TRY.
      cl_salv_table=>factory(
      EXPORTING
      r_container = lo_cont_1

IMPORTING r_salv_table = lo_alv_1
      CHANGING
      t_table  = ut_cust_early ).
      cl_salv_table=>factory(
EXPORTING
      r_container = lo_cont_2
IMPORTING
      r_salv_table = lo_alv_2
CHANGING
      t_table  = ut_cust_late ).
lo_alv_1->display( ).
lo_alv_2->display( ).
CALL SCREEN 0100.
CATCH cx_salv_msg INTO lo_msg.
MESSAGE lo_msg TYPE 'I'.
LEAVE LIST-PROCESSING.
ENDTRY.
```

```
ENDFORM.        "display
*&--------------------------------------------------------------*
*&       Module STATUS_0100    OUTPUT
*&--------------------------------------------------------------*
•        text
*----------------------------------------------------------------*
MODULE status_0100 OUTPUT.
SET PF-STATUS 'STATUS_0100'.
SET TITLEBAR 'TITLE_0100'.


ENDMODULE.    " STATUS_0100  OUTPUT
*&--------------------------------------------------------------*
*&       Module USER_COMMAND_0100        INPUT
*&--------------------------------------------------------------*
• text

*----------------------------------------------------------------*
MODULE user_command_0100 INPUT.

save_ok_code = ok_code.
CLEAR ok_code.
CASE save_ok_code.

WHEN 'BACK'.
LEAVE TO SCREEN 0.
WHEN 'EXIT'.
LEAVE PROGRAM.
ENDCASE.
ENDMODULE.    " USER_COMMAND_0100        INPUT
```

8. CDS (Core Data Services) Views

Creating HANA Views (Attribute, Analytic and Calculation) involves creating HANA artifacts in the HANA database layer (from SAP HANA Modeler perspective). These views are then consumed in our ABAP reports either through ADBC, or External Views. Hence this is a ***BOTTOM-UP approach***. Such BOTTOM-UP approach is not recommended because of the difficulty in creating and transporting the HANA artifacts (through Delivery Units). In case any underlying HANA artifact is not included in the Transport (via Delivery Unit and Transport Container), then there will not be any errors reported at the time of releasing the Transports.

For this reason, SAP recommends the ***TOP-DOWN approach***. The TOP-DOWN approach equivalent to creation of HANA views, is CDS (Core Data Services) Views. These are created from the ABAP perspective, can be saved directly in a TR, and consumed in ABAP reports through Open SQL.

Creating CDS Views

In the following example, we will create a CDS View that takes as input the Client, a Target Currency, and a Date, and returns the list of all Customers who have booked flights before the Input Date, and their Booking Amounts converted to the Target Currency.

[<u>Note</u>: The following are not yet supported in CDS Views:

(a)   Aggregation (SUM, AVG, etc) of some CURRENCY_CONVERSION or UNIT_ CONVERSION

(b)   SELECT TOP N

(c)   ORDER BY

(d)   Nested use of CAST]

Step 1: Ensure that you are in the ABAP perspective (if not already). Right-click on your Package and follow the menu-path New Other ABAP Repository Object Dictionary DDL Source. Press NEXT.

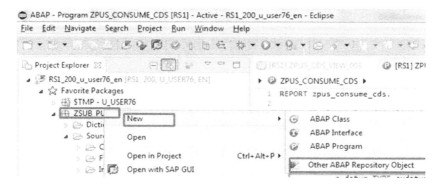

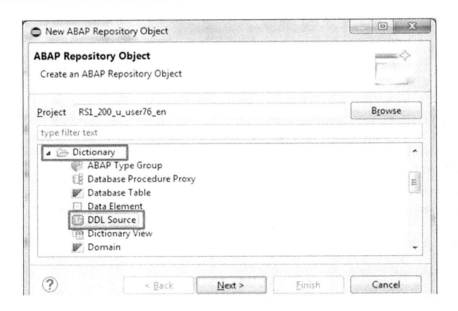

Step 2: Enter a Name and Description. Press NEXT.

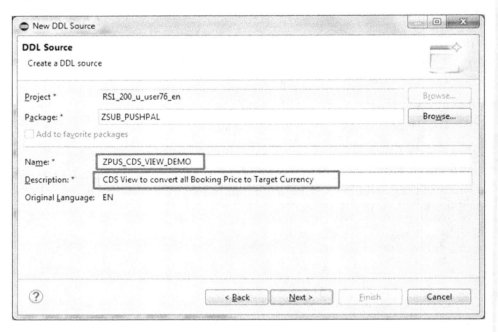

Step 3: Select a TR to save the CDS View. Press NEXT.

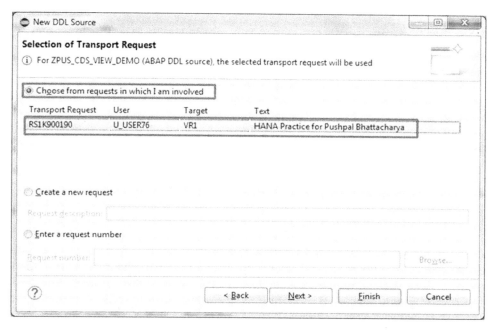

Step 4: In the next screen, several pre-defined templates for CDs Views are provided. In this particular example, we will select "Define View with Parameters". Press FINISH.

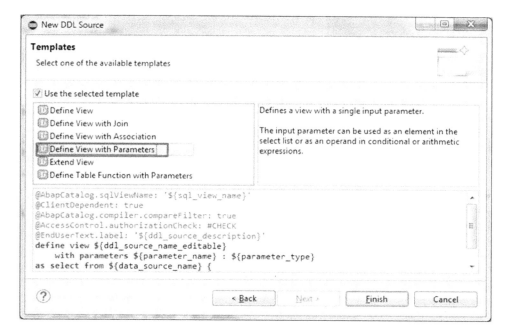

Step 5: The following template CDS View will be displayed. In this window, we will have to write our code.

Note that this code is neither in Open SQL, nor in Native SQL. It is in a language that is specific to CDS only.

It does not support all the Native SQL features either.

```
[RS1] ZPUS_CDS_VIEW_003     [RS1] ZPUS_CONSUME_CDS     [RS1] ZPUS_HA400_EX1     *[RS1] ZPUS
  1  @AbapCatalog.sqlViewName: sql_view_name
  2  @ClientDependent: true
  3  @AbapCatalog.compiler.compareFilter: true
  4  @AccessControl.authorizationCheck: #CHECK
  5  @EndUserText.label: 'CDS View to convert all Booking Price to Target Currency'
  6  define view Zpus_Cds_View_Demo
  7      with parameters parameter_name : parameter_type
  8  as select from data_source_name {
  9
 10  }
```

Step 6: First, we need to specify a SQL_VIEW_NAME (as highlighted in the above screen. Note that whenever we activate a CDS view, a DDIC View is created in the ABAP Data dictionary. Hence this SQL View Name must follow all the naming standards and conventions of ABAP DDIC Views.

```
[RS1] ZPUS_CDS_VIEW_003     [RS1] ZPUS_CONSUME_CDS     [RS1] ZPUS_HA400_EX1     *[R:
  1  @AbapCatalog.sqlViewName: 'ZPUS_CDS_DDIC'
  2  @ClientDependent: true
  3  @AbapCatalog.compiler.compareFilter: true
  4  @AccessControl.authorizationCheck: #CHECK
  5  @EndUserText.label: 'CDS View to convert all Booking Price to Target Currency'
  6  define view Zpus_Cds_View_Demo
  7      with parameters parameter_name : parameter_type
  8  as select from data_source_name {
  9
 10  }
```

Step 7: Write the code as shown below. Note how the Input Parameters (and their data-types) are declared.

```
[RS1] ZPUS_CDS_VIEW_DEMO
 1  @AbapCatalog.sqlViewName: 'ZPUS_CDS_DDIC'
 2  @ClientDependent: true
 3  @AbapCatalog.compiler.CompareFilter: true
 4  @AccessControl.authorizationCheck: #CHECK
 5  @EndUserText.label: 'CDS View to convert all Booking Price to Target Currency'
 6  define view Zpus_Cds_View_Demo
 7      with parameters p_mandt : S_MANDT,          Input Parameters with Data-type
 8                      p_flights_before : S_BDATE, (data-elements allowed)
 9                      p_to_curr : S_CURR
10  as select from scustom as c inner join sbook as b   JOIN Tables
11  on c.mandt = b.mandt and c.id = b.customid      JOIN Conditions
12  {
13      c.id,
14      c.name,
15      c.postcode,          Comma-separated Field-list without Aliases
16      c.city,
17      c.country,
18      currency_conversion(
19        amount => b.forcuram,
20        source_currency => b.forcurkey,
21        target_currency => :p_to_curr,
22        exchange_rate_date => b.order_date,  Currency Conversion function
23        exchange_rate_type => 'M',
24        client => :p_mandt,
25        round => 'X',
26        error_handling => 'SET_TO_NULL'
27      ) as amt_to_curr,
28      :p_to_curr as to_curr       Fixed Column with Alias
29  }
30  where c.mandt = :p_mandt
31    and b.order_date < :p_flights_before;   Input Parameters in WHERE-clause
32
```

Step 8: Save and Activate the CDS View. This will also create a DDIC View with the specified name.

Creating and Consuming SAP HANA Artifacts and ABAP Artifacts for SAP HANA

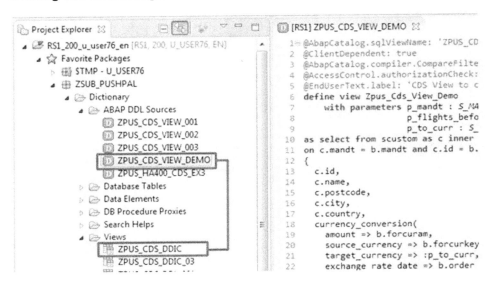

Step 9: To test the CDS view, right-click on the CDS view and select "Open Data Preview". Since this CDS View has Input Parameters, it will prompt for the Inputs.

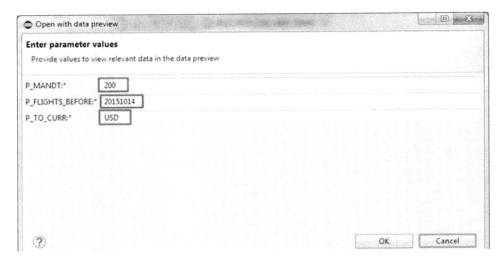

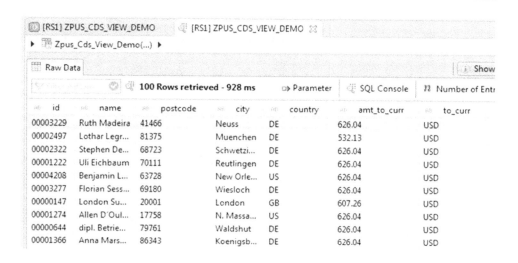

Consuming CDS View

CDS Views can be consumed from ABAP Reports using New Open SQL with comma-separated Input Parameters (if any) specified within parenthesis immediately after the CDS View name.

In the following example, we will consume the CDS View created in Creating CDS Views to list the Top N Customers having highest sum total of Booking Amounts for flights before an Input Date.

🖃 Output

Consume CDS View with Input Parameters

ID	NAME	POSTCODE	CITY	COUNTRY	AMT_TOT	TO_CURR
00001450	Anne-Marie Waldmann	90419	Nuernberg	DE	33465.76	USD
00004089	Friedrich Benjamin	63263	Neu-Isenburg	DE	31717.29	USD
00001033	Anneliese Meier	23056	Buxtehude	DE	31695.92	USD
00001178	Benjamin Dumbach	63728	New Orleans	US	31367.02	USD
00004501	Thilo Sisko	23496	Dielheim	DE	30980.62	USD
00001198	Florian Kramer	69180	Wiesloch	DE	30797.91	USD
00000332	Thilo Vrsic	23496	Dielheim	DE	30651.72	USD
00004369	Guillermo Hoffen	28020	Madrid	ES	30506.3	USD
00000056	Blacks AG	66000	Frankfurt/Main	DE	30359.44	USD
00000484	Ida Gueldenpfennig	66386	St. Ingbert	DE	30218.64	USD

The following is the source-code for this report:

REPORT zpus_consume_cds_demo.

* Selection-Screen Definition
PARAMETERS: p_to_c   TYPE s_curr,   " Target Currency

               p_num   TYPE int4,   " No. of Customers

               p_datum   TYPE sydatum.   " Flights Before

* Database Access
START-OF-SELECTION.

* First Check if Views With Parameters is supported IF cl_abap_dbfeatures=>use_
features(

                     ˙EXPORTING

                     requested_features = VALUE #((

cl_abap_dbfeatures=>views_with_parameters))

).

* Consume CDS View
SELECT id,

               name,

               postcode,

               city,

               country,

               SUM(amt_to_curr) AS amt_tot,

               to_curr

```
                    UP TO @p_num ROWS
                    FROM zpus_cds_ddic( p_mandt  = @sy-mandt,
                              p_flights_before  = @p_datum,
                              p_to_curr         = @p_to_c )
                    INTO TABLE @DATA(lt_customers)
                    GROUP BY id, name, postcode, city, country, to_curr
                    ORDER BY amt_tot DESCENDING.
ENDIF.
```

```
* Output Display
  END-OF-SELECTION.
  IF NOT lt_customers IS INITIAL.
```

```
* Display Output
  cl_demo_output=>display_data( value = lt_customers
              name      = 'Consume CDS View with Input Parameters' ).
ENDIF.
```

9. ABAP Managed Database Procedure (AMDP)

Similar to HANA Views (Attribute, Analytic and Calculation), creating Stored Procedures also involve creating HANA artifacts in the HANA database layer (from SAP HANA Modeler perspective). These Stored Procedures are then consumed in our ABAP reports either through ADBC, or through Database Procedure Proxy. Hence this is a ***BOTTOM-UP approach***. Such BOTTOM-UP approach is not recommended because of the difficulty in creating and transporting the HANA artifacts (through Delivery Units). In case any underlying HANA artifact is not included in the Transport (via Delivery Unit and Transport Container), then there will not be any errors reported at the time of releasing the Transports.

For this reason, SAP recommends the ***TOP-DOWN approach***. The TOP-DOWN approach equivalent to creation of Stored Procedure, is AMDP (ABAP Managed Database Procedure). This is basically an ABAP Class (created from the ABAP perspective) that includes an interface IF_AMDP_MARKER_HDB, can be saved directly in a TR, and consumed in ABAP reports through a Method call.

Creating AMDP

AMDP Classes can be created only in ADT. It can only be displayed from the Class Builder of SAP GUI through T/Code SE24, but not created or modified. Also, the Native SQL syntax written inside the AMDP Method is exactly similar to that written inside Store Procedure.

In this section, we will create an AMDP that does exactly the same function as the Stored Procedure created above. The AMDP will retrieve the first N and last N Customers from the Attribute View created above, based on their Average Days Ahead Bookings. The value of N will be determined by an Input Parameter IM_NUMBER. Also, the client will be determined by another Input Parameter IM_CLIENT. This Procedure will return 2 result-sets having the same structure.

Step 1: Ensure that you are in the ABAP perspective (if not already). Right-click on your Package and follow the menu-path New ABAP Class.

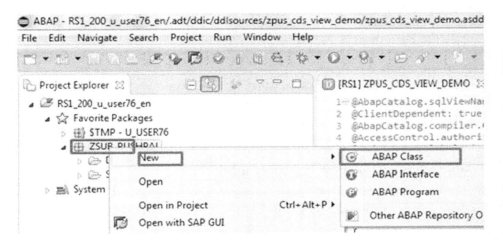

Step 2: Enter the Name and Description of the AMDP Class. Press NEXT.

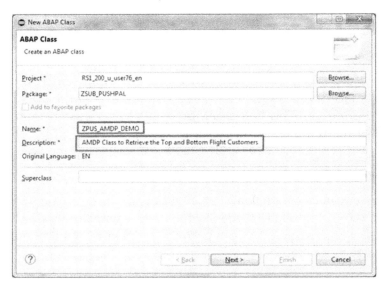

Step 3: Select the Transport and click FINISH.

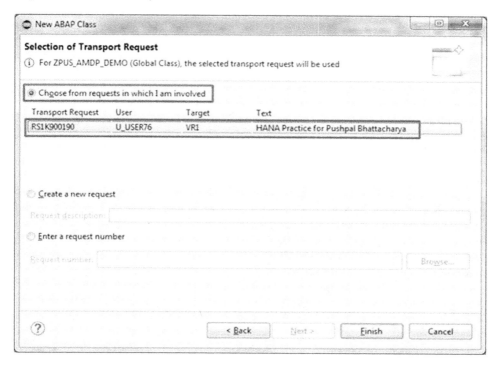

Step 4: The following template will be presented wherein we will have to write the AMDP Class Definition as well as the Methods Implementation.

```
@ [RS1] ZPUS_AMDP_DEMO 23   @ [RS1] ZPUS_HA400_CL_A
▶ @ ZPUS_AMDP_DEMO ▶
 1  CLASS zpus_amdp_demo DEFINITION
 2    PUBLIC
 3    FINAL
 4    CREATE PUBLIC .
 5
 6  PUBLIC SECTION.
 7  PROTECTED SECTION.
 8  PRIVATE SECTION.
 9  ENDCLASS.
10
11
12
13  CLASS zpus_amdp_demo IMPLEMENTATION.
14  ENDCLASS.
```

Step 5: The first step is to include the Interface IF_AMDP_MARKER_HDB. Write the code as shown below.

```
CLASS zpus_amdp_demo DEFINITION
        PUBLIC
        FINAL
        CREATE PUBLIC .
        PUBLIC SECTION.
* Mandatory Interface Declaration INTERFACES
        if_amdp_marker_hdb.

* Structure for Results
        TYPES: BEGIN OF ly_output,

id                TYPE s_customer,
name              TYPE s_custname,
postcode          TYPE postcode,
city              TYPE  city,
country           TYPE  s_country,
avg_days_ahead TYPE int4,
END OF ly_output.

* Table Type for Results
TYPES ly_t_output TYPE STANDARD TABLE OF ly_output.

* AMDP Method to Retrieve Early and Late Flight Customers METHODS
  meth_get_early_late
        IMPORTING VALUE(im_number) TYPE i
                  VALUE(im_client)              TYPE symandt
                  EXPORTING VALUE(et_early)     TYPE ly_t_output
                  VALUE(et_late)                TYPE ly_t_output.


PROTECTED SECTION.
PRIVATE SECTION.
ENDCLASS.

CLASS zpus_amdp_demo IMPLEMENTATION.
```

```
METHOD meth_get_early_late BY DATABASE PROCEDURE FOR HDB
                           LANGUAGE SQLSCRIPT
                           OPTIONS READ-ONLY
                           USING scustom
                           sbook.
```

* Select List of Top Customers with Highest Average Days Ahead et_early =
  select top :im_number
      c.id, c.name, c.postcode, c.city, c.country,
      AVG(DAYS_BETWEEN(TO_DATE(b.order_date, 'YYYYMMDD'), TO_DATE(b. fldate, 'YYYYMMDD')))
                  as avg_days_ahead
      from scustom as c inner join sbook as b
      on c.mandt = b.mandt and c.id = b.customid
      where c.mandt = :im_client
      group by c.mandt, c.id, c.name, c.postcode, c.city, c.country order by avg_ days_ahead desc;

* Select List of Top Customers with Lowest Average Days Ahead et_late =
  select top :im_number
      c.id, c.name, c.postcode, c.city, c.country,
      AVG(DAYS_BETWEEN(TO_DATE(b.order_date, 'YYYYMMDD'), TO_DATE(b. fldate, 'YYYYMMDD')))
      as avg_days_ahead
      from scustom as c inner join sbook as b
      on c.mandt = b.mandt and c.id = b.customid
      where c.mandt = :im_client
      group by c.mandt, c.id, c.name, c.postcode, c.city, c.country order by avg_ days_ahead asc;

ENDMETHOD.

ENDCLASS.

Step 6: Activate the AMDP Class. The AMDP Class Method can now be tested normally from the ABAP Class Builder (with T/Code SE24).

Consuming AMD

To consume the AMDP that we created in Creating AMDP, we will write a report that is very similar to that written in Consuming Stored Procedures)

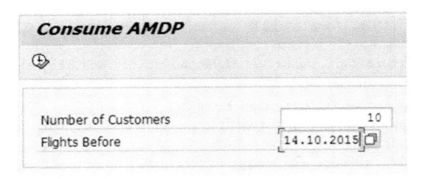

Cust. No.	Customer name	Postal Code	City	Co...	Number
2147	Thilo Jacqmain	23496	Dielheim	DE	191
4182	Florian Heller	69180	Wiesloch	DE	181
2483	Cindy Kramer	76018	Arlington	US	176
1581	Fabio Montero	00195	Roma	IT	176
3594	Thomas Pratt	60657	Chicago	US	172
4179	Amelie Domenech	68753	Amelie	DE	172
3845	Salvador Goelke	41006	Sevilla	ES	171
674	Astrid Jacqmain	68219	Mannheim	DE	169
212	Werk 1200 Dresden	10069	Dresden	DE	169
1921	Juan Hansmann	28017	Madrid	ES	168

Cust. No.	Customer name	Postal Code	City	Co...	Number
3622	Holm Meier	69121	Heidelberg	DE	14
3960	Adam Buchholm	69483	Wald-Michelbach	DE	14
3621	Anna Wohl	86343	Koenigsbrunn	DE	15
1472	Lothar Kreiss	69180	Walldorf	DE	15
4076	Ruth Neubasler	41466	Neuss	DE	15
3056	Marta Madeira	08014	Barcelona	ES	16
4299	Salvador Delon	41006	Sevilla	ES	17
1590	Christine Lindwurm	68163	Mannheim	DE	18
2152	Sophie Kirk	67105	Schifferstadt	DE	18
2378	August Jacqmain	66464	Homburg	DE	19

Given below is the source-code for this report.

```
REPORT zpus_consume_amdp.

* Tables for results
DATA: gt_cust_early    TYPE    zpus_amdp_
      demo=>ly_t_output,    gt_cust_late
      TYPE      zpus_amdp_demo=>ly_t_
      output.

* Screen processing
DATA: ok_code         TYPE syucomm,

      save_ok_code TYPE syucomm.

* selection       screen
SELECTION-SCREEN  BEGIN OF BLOCK cus WITH FRAME TITLE text-cus.
PARAMETERS: p_num  TYPE  i DEFAULT 10, " Number of Customers
                p_date TYPE sydatum.        " Flights Before
SELECTION-SCREEN  END OF BLOCK cus.

START-OF-SELECTION.

        PERFORM get_data
    CHANGING gt_cust_early

              gt_cust_late.

    PERFORM display
    USING gt_cust_early

          gt_cust_late.
*&---------------------------------------------------------------------*
*&        Form    GET_DATA
*&---------------------------------------------------------------------*
FORM get_data CHANGING ct_cust_early TYPE zpus_amdp_demo=>ly_t_output

                    ct_cust_late    TYPE zpus_amdp_demo=>ly_t_
                    output.

  CLEAR: ct_cust_early,

          ct_cust_late.

* Call AMDP Method to retrieve Early Bird/
  Late Customers NEW zpus_amdp_demo(
  )->meth_get_early_late(
```

```
                    EXPORTING
                      im_number = p_num
                      im_client = sy-mandt
                    IMPORTING
                      et_early    = ct_cust_early
                      et_late     = ct_cust_late ).


ENDFORM. " GET_DATA
*&-------------------------------------------------------------------*
*&        Form    output
*&-------------------------------------------------------------------*
FORM display USING ut_cust_early TYPE zpus_amdp_demo=>ly_t_output
                   ut_cust_late  TYPE zpus_amdp_demo=>ly_t_output.
    DATA: lo_cont_1 TYPE REF TO cl_gui_custom_container,
          lo_cont_2 TYPE REF TO cl_gui_custom_container,
        lo_alv_1     TYPE REF TO cl_salv_table,
        lo_alv_2     TYPE REF TO cl_salv_table,
        lo_msg       TYPE REF TO cx_salv_msg.
*   create containers CREATE OBJECT lo_cont_1
      EXPORTING
    container_name      =   'UPPER_AREA'
    repid               =   sy-repid
    dynnr               = '0100'
  EXCEPTIONS
    OTHERS              =   1.
  IF sy-subrc <> 0.
    MESSAGE i398(00) WITH 'Error Creating Container Control'.
    LEAVE LIST-PROCESSING.
  ENDIF.
  CREATE OBJECT lo_cont_2
      EXPORTING
```

```
container_name   =  'LOWER_AREA'
repid            =  sy-repid
dynnr            = '0100'
EXCEPTIONS
  OTHERS         =  1.
  IF sy-subrc <> 0.
    MESSAGE i398(00) WITH 'Error Creating Container Control'.
    LEAVE LIST-PROCESSING.
  ENDIF.

* create salv grid controls TRY.
      cl_salv_table=>factory(
          EXPORTING
             r_container = lo_cont_1
          IMPORTING r_salv_table = lo_alv_1
          CHANGING
             t_table        = ut_cust_early ).
      cl_salv_table=>factory(
          EXPORTING
             r_container = lo_cont_2
          IMPORTING
             r_salv_table = lo_alv_2
          CHANGING
             t_table        = ut_cust_late ).
      lo_alv_1->display( ).
      lo_alv_2->display( ).
      CALL SCREEN 0100.
    CATCH cx_salv_msg INTO lo_msg.
      MESSAGE lo_msg TYPE 'I'.
      LEAVE LIST-PROCESSING.
  ENDTRY.
ENDFORM.          "display
*&---------------------------------------------------------------*
*&      Module  STATUS_0100  OUTPUT
```

```
*&---------------------------------------------------------------*
*  text
*---------------------------------------------------------------*
MODULE status_0100 OUTPUT.
   SET PF-STATUS 'STATUS_0100'.
   SET TITLEBAR 'TITLE_0100'.

ENDMODULE.      " STATUS_0100 OUTPUT


*&---------------------------------------------------------------*
*&         Module   USER_COMMAND_0100          INPUT
*&---------------------------------------------------------------*
*  text

*---------------------------------------------------------------* MODULE user_
command_0100 INPUT.
   save_ok_code = ok_code.
   CLEAR ok_code.
   CASE save_ok_code.
     WHEN 'BACK'.
       LEAVE TO SCREEN 0.
     WHEN 'EXIT'.
       LEAVE PROGRAM.
   ENDCASE.
ENDMODULE.      " USER_COMMAND_0100      INPUT
```

10. ALV for HANA

In the following example, we will create an ALV for HANA that displays the details of all Customers who had booked a Flight in the input date range. The Booking amounts are displayed in the original booking currency, as well as in a fixed Target currency.

For the above, we will first create a CDS view that fetches all the details from the database tables SCUSTOM and SBOOK, and also performs the Currency conversion (based on Input Parameter). Thereafter, we will consume this CDS view inside our ABAP Report program to display ALV for HANA.

Note:

(a)   As of now, ALV for HANA can be displayed only for CDS Views, DDIC Views or DDIC tables and no other artifacts

(b)   The example shown below pertains to ALV for HANA for CDS View wherein the method CL_SALV_GUI_TABLE_IDA=>CREATE_FOR_CDS_VIEW has been used. For DDIC tables and Views, use the method CL_SALV_GUI_TABLE_IDA=>CREATE. Everything else remain the same.

(c)   For CDS Views, Text based Search is currently not supported in ALV for HANA. It can only be implemented for Tables that specifically has "Column Store" radio-button selected.

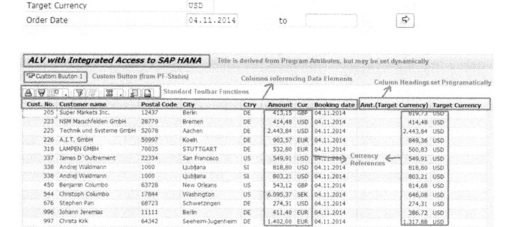

Following is the CDS View created to fetch the data:

```
@AbapCatalog.sqlViewName: 'ZPUS_CDS_DDIC_04'
@ClientDependent: true
@AbapCatalog.compiler.CompareFilter: true
    @AccessControl.authorizationCheck: #CHECK
    @EndUserText.label: 'Convert all Flight
    Booking Amounts to USD' define view
    Zpus_Cds_Alv_Demo
  with parameters
    p_mandt : S_
        MANDT,
    p_to_curr : S_
        CURR
      as select from scustom
      as c inner join sbook
      as b on c.mandt =
      b.mandt and c.id =
      b.customid
      {
        c.id,
        c.name,
        c.postcode,
        c.city,
        c.country,
        b.forcuram,
        b.forcurkey,
        b.order_date,
        currency_conversion(
          amount => b.forcuram,
          source_currency => b.forcurkey,
          target_currency => :p_to_curr,
          exchange_rate_date => b.order_date,
          exchange_rate_type => 'M',
          client => :p_mandt,
          round => 'X',
          error_handling => 'SET_TO_NULL'
        ) as amt_to_curr,
        :p_to_curr as to_curr
```

```
            }
                where c.mandt = :p_mandt;
```

Following is the source-code extract for the ABAP report that consumes the above CDS View to display ALV for

HANA:

```
REPORT zpus_alv_with_cds_demo.

* Selection-screen
DATA: gv_order_date TYPE s_bdate.
PARAMETERS: p_to_cur
TYPE s_curr. " Target
Currency SELECT-OPTIONS
s_date FOR gv_order_date.
" Order Date

CLASS lcl_alv_fullscreen DEFINITION FINAL.
  PUBLIC SECTION.
    METHODS display.
    METHODS status_function_selected
                  FOR EVENT function_selected
      OF if_salv_gui_fullscreen_ida IMPORTING
      ev_fcode.
  PRIVATE SECTION.

*     Function-Code for Custom Button
      CONSTANTS lc_flag_fcode TYPE ui_func VALUE 'BUT1'.
*     Declarations for HANA ALV
      DATA lo_salv TYPE REF TO if_salv_gui_table_ida.

ENDCLASS.
CLASS lcl_alv_fullscreen IMPLEMENTATION.

  METHOD display.

*    **** Step 1: Create ALV Instance ****
      TRY.
```

```
        CALL METHOD cl_salv_gui_table_ida=>create_for_cds_view
          EXPORTING
            iv_cds_view_name        = 'ZPUS_CDS_ALV_DEMO'
          RECEIVING
            ro_alv_gui_table_ida = lo_salv.


*    **** Step 2: Restrict Data Display based on Order Date in Selection-Screen
     ****
        PERFORM sub_sel_screen_filter USING lo_salv.


*    **** Step 3: Field-Catalog Modifications ****
        PERFORM sub_modify_fcat USING lo_salv.


*    **** Step 4: Set View Parameters (if CDS View has Input Parameters) ****
        PERFORM sub_set_view_params USING lo_salv.


*    **** Step 5: Set PF-Status ****
        PERFORM sub_set_pf_status USING lo_salv.
        SET HANDLER status_function_selected FOR lo_salv->fullscreen( ).


*    **** Step 6: Set Zebra Pattern of ALV ****
        lo_salv->display_options( )->enable_alternating_row_pattern( ).


*    **** Step 7: Set the Text for empty table ****
        lo_salv->display_options(
        )->set_empty_table_text( 'No
        Records found for specified
        condition'(e01) ).


*    **** Step 8: Display ALV in Full-screen ****
        lo_salv->fullscreen( )->display( ).


*        CATCH cx_salv_db_connection .
*        CATCH cx_salv_db_table_not_supported .
*        CATCH cx_salv_ida_contract_violation .
*        CATCH cx_salv_function_not_supported .
```

```
    ENDTRY.

    ENDMETHOD.

* Handler
  Method
  for Buttons
  pressed
  METHOD
  status_
  function_
  selected.
     CASE ev_fcode.
       WHEN lc_flag_fcode.
         MESSAGE i000(0k) WITH 'Button Flag pressed!'(i01).
       WHEN OTHERS.
          lo_salv->fullscreen( )->exit( ).
     ENDCASE.
    ENDMETHOD.
ENDCLASS.

END-OF-SELECTION.
* Call Method to Display ALV
   NEW lcl_alv_fullscreen( )->display( ).
*&-------------------------------------------------------------------*
*&      Form   SUB_SEL_SCREEN_FILTER
*&-------------------------------------------------------------------*
*         Restrict Data Display based on Order Date in Selection-Screen
*-------------------------------------------------------------------* FORM
sub_sel_screen_filter USING uo_salv TYPE REF TO if_salv_gui_
table_ida.
    DATA: lo_range_collector TYPE REF TO cl_salv_range_tab_collector,
          lt_ranges                TYPE if_salv_service_types=>yt_named_ranges.

* Step 2a) Create Instance of Range Table Collector CREATE OBJECT lo_range_
  collector.
```

```
* Step 2b) Add the Range Table Filters
  CALL METHOD lo_range_collector->add_ranges_for_name
  EXPORTING

       iv_name = 'ORDER_DATE' it_ranges = s_date[].


* Step 2c) Get the Collected Range to be passed on to ALV CALL METHOD lo_
  range_collector->get_collected_ranges
     IMPORTING
        et_named_ranges = lt_ranges.


* Step 2d) Set the Select Options
  CALL METHOD uo_salv->set_select_options
     EXPORTING
        it_ranges = lt_ranges.


ENDFORM.
*&---------------------------------------------------------------*
*&          Form   SUB_MODIFY_FCAT
*&---------------------------------------------------------------*
*           Field-Catalog Modifications


*-------------------------------------------------------------* FORM sub_modify_fcat
USING uo_salv TYPE REF TO if_salv_gui_table_ida.
    DATA lo_field_catalog TYPE REF TO if_salv_gui_field_catalog_ida.


* Step 3a) Display attributes of table fields (interface)
    CALL METHOD uo_salv->field_catalog
       RECEIVING
          ro_field_catalog = lo_field_catalog.


* Step 3b) Reference Data Elements for ALV Columns PERFORM sub_ref_data_
  elements USING lo_field_catalog.


* Step 3c) Change Column Headings for non-DDIC fields PERFORM sub_set_
  field_header_text USING lo_field_catalog.
* Step 3d) Set Currency Reference Fields for Amount Columns PERFORM sub_
```

```
      set_currency_ref USING lo_field_catalog.

ENDFORM.

*&-------------------------------------------------------------*
*&        Form   SUB_REF_DATA_ELEMENTS
*&-------------------------------------------------------------*
*         Reference Data Elements for ALV Columns

 *-------------------------------------------------
                                                              *
 ----------------
   FORM sub_ref_data_elements  USING uo_field_catalog TYPE REF TO if_salv_
                               gui_field_catalog_ida.
* Set data description of a field by a data element
      PERFORM sub_set_data_element
      USING:
                uo_field_catalog 'ID'          'S_CUSTOMER',
                uo_field_catalog 'NAME'        'S_CUSTNAME',
                uo_field_catalog 'POSTCODE'    'POSTCODE',
                uo_field_catalog 'CITY'        'CITY',
                uo_field_catalog 'COUNTRY'     'S_COUNTRY',
                uo_field_catalog 'FORCURAM'    'S_F_CUR_PR',
                uo_field_catalog 'FORCURKEY'   'S_CURR',
                uo_field_catalog 'ORDER_       'S_BDATE'.
                                 DATE'
ENDFORM.

*&        -------------------------------------------------------------
                                                              *
*&              Form  SUB_SET_DATA_ELEMENT
*&        -------------------------------------------------------------
                                                              *

* Set data description of a field by a data element
*-------------------------------------------------------------*
FORM sub_set_data_element USING uo_field_catalog               TYPE
REF TO
if_salv_gui_field_catalog_ida
```

                                        VALUE(uv_field_name)   TYPE
if_salv_gui_types_ida=>y_field_name
                                        VALUE(uv_data_element_name) TYPE
if_salv_gui_types_ida=>y_data_element_name.

* Set data description of a field by a data element CALL METHOD uo_field_
  catalog->set_data_element
    EXPORTING
      iv_field_name   = uv_field_name
      iv_data_element_name = uv_data_element_name.

ENDFORM.

```
*&---------------------------------------------------------------------*
*&      Form   SUB_SET_FIELD_HEADER_TEXT
*&---------------------------------------------------------------------*
*       Change Column Headings for non-DDIC fields
*----------------------------------------------------------------------*
```

FORM sub_set_field_header_text USING uo_field_catalog TYPE REF TO if_salv_
gui_field_catalog_ida.

* Set Field Header Texts for Columns that do not reference Data Elements
  PERFORM sub_set_header_text USING:

          uo_field_catalog 'AMT_TO_CURR' 'Amt.(Target Currency)'(h01),
          uo_field_catalog 'TO_CURR'   'Target Currency'(h02).

ENDFORM.
```
*&---------------------------------------------------------------------*
*&      Form   SUB_SET_HEADER_TEXT
*&---------------------------------------------------------------------*
*       Set Field Headers for Columns that dont refer Data Elements
*----------------------------------------------------------------------*
```
FORM sub_set_header_text USING uo_field_catalog   TYPE REF TO
if_salv_gui_field_catalog_ida
                                        VALUE(uv_field_name) TYPE if_salv_gui_
                                        types_ida=>y_field_name VALUE(uv_
                                        header_text) TYPE if_salv_gui_types_

```
                                   ida=>y_header_text.

* Set Field Header Texts for Columns
  CALL METHOD uo_field_catalog->set_field_header_texts
    EXPORTING
      iv_field_name = uv_field_name iv_header_text = uv_header_text.


ENDFORM.
*&---------------------------------------------------------------------*
*&      Form   SUB_SET_CURRENCY_REF
*&---------------------------------------------------------------------*
*          Set Currency Reference Fields for Amount Columns
*----------------------------------------------------------------------*
FORM sub_set_currency_ref USING uo_field_catalog TYPE REF TO if_salv_gui_
field_catalog_ida.


* Set Currency
  Reference Fields for
  Amount Columns
  PERFORM sub_set_
  curr_ref USING:
          uo_field_catalog 'FORCURAM'          'FORCURKEY',
          uo_field_catalog 'AMT_TO_CURR' 'TO_CURR'.


ENDFORM.
*&---------------------------------------------------------------------*
*&      Form   SUB_SET_CURR_REF
*&---------------------------------------------------------------------*
*          Set Currency Reference Fields for Amount Columns
*----------------------------------------------------------------------*
*          -->P_UO_FIELD_CATALOG  text
*          -->P_0324      text
*          -->P_0325      text
*----------------------------------------------------------------------*
FORM sub_set_curr_ref USING uo_field_catalog                    TYPE REF
TO
if_salv_gui_field_catalog_ida
                                   VALUE(uv_amount_field_name)    TYPE
if_salv_gui_types_ida=>y_field_name
```

VALUE(uv_currency_field_name) TYPE if_salv_gui_types_ida=>y_field_name.

```
* Set Currency Reference Fields for Amount Columns
   CALL METHOD uo_field_catalog->set_currency_reference_field
     EXPORTING
       iv_amount_field_name   = uv_amount_field_name
       iv_currency_field_name = uv_currency_field_name.

ENDFORM.
*&---------------------------------------------------------------------*
*&       Form   SUB_SET_VIEW_PARAMS
*&---------------------------------------------------------------------*
*        Set View Parameters (if CDS View has Input Parameters)
*----------------------------------------------------------* FORM sub_set_view_
params USING uo_salv TYPE REF TO if_salv_gui_table_ida.
   DATA lt_parameters TYPE if_salv_gui_types_ida=>yt_parameter.
* Step 4a) Collect all View Parameters PERFORM sub_collect_view_params:
               USING 'P_MANDT'    sy-mandt CHANGING lt_parameters,
               USING 'P_TO_CURR' p_to_cur CHANGING lt_parameters.

* Step 4b) Set values for placeholder variables in the database view CALL
   METHOD uo_salv->set_view_parameters
     EXPORTING
       it_parameters = lt_parameters.
ENDFORM.
*&---------------------------------------------------------------------*
*&       Form   SUB_COLLECT_VIEW_PARAMS
*&---------------------------------------------------------------------*
*        Collect all View Parameters
*----------------------------------------------------------------------*
FORM sub_collect_view_params USING       VALUE(uv_name) TYPE string
                                         uv_value          TYPE any
CHANGING ct_parameters                                TYPE if_salv_gui_types_
                                                       ida=>yt_parameter.
   FIELD-SYMBOLS: <lfs_parameters> TYPE if_salv_gui_types_ida=>ys_
   parameter.
   APPEND INITIAL LINE TO ct_parameters ASSIGNING <lfs_parameters>.
   <lfs_parameters>-name    = uv_name.
   <lfs_parameters>-value = uv_value.
```

UNASSIGN <lfs_parameters>.

ENDFORM.

```
*&--------------------------------------------------------------------*
*&          Form    SUB_SET_PF_STATUS
*&--------------------------------------------------------------------*
*           Set PF-Status
*--------------------------------------------------------------------* FORM sub_set_pf_
status USING uo_salv TYPE REF TO if_salv_gui_table_ida.
    CALL METHOD uo_salv->fullscreen( )->set_pf_status(
        iv_pf_status_name = 'STANDARD1'
        iv_program_name   = sy-repid ).
```

ENDFORM.

Following is the screenshot of the PF-STATUS created for the above program:

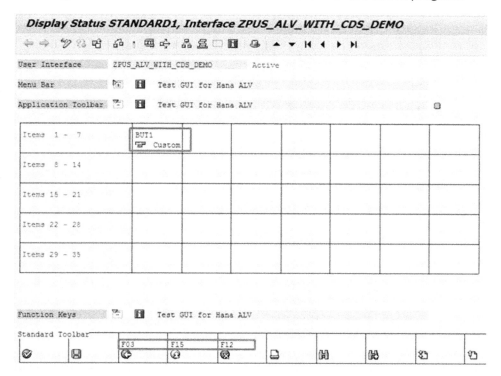

6.12 Sample Exercises with Solutions for Practice and Hands-on

Exercise 1: Create and Consume Stored Procedure without Currency Conversion

Requirement:

In EPM Model the sales order tables are as below:

SNWD_SO (Header), SNWD_SO_I (Item), SNWD_BPA (Business Partner)

Tables SNWD_SO & SNWD_BPA are linked by SNWD_SO. BUYER_GUID = SNWD_BPA. NODE_KEY

We need to find out the Business Partners (SNWD_BPA. BP_ID) and the Gross Total Order Value (SNWD_SO.

GROSS_AMOUNT) of these BP.

List out the Top N Business Partners with descending order of Gross Order Value.

Write a Stored Procedure taking the N as input parameter and it will export list of Top N BP & Corresponding Gross Order Value in descending order.

Call this Stored Procedure from an ABAP Report and display the list in a classical report output.

Assumption – All the sales order Gross amount values are in same currency.

Solution:

Created the following Stored Procedure:

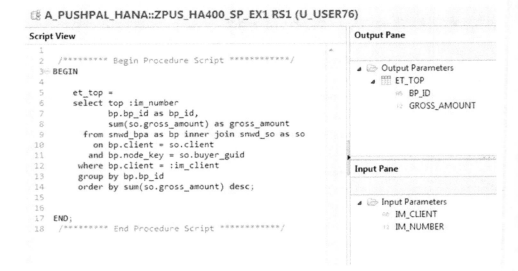

🗐 A_PUSHPAL_HANA::ZPUS_HA400_SP_EX1 RS1 (U_USER76)

Script View	Output Pane
1	
2 /********* Begin Procedure Script ***********/	▲ ⬡ Output Parameters
3 BEGIN	▲ ⊞ ET_TOP
4	BP_ID
5 et_top =	GROSS_AMOUNT
6 select top :im_number	
7 bp.bp_id as bp_id,	
8 sum(so.gross_amount) as gross_amount	
9 from snwd_bpa as bp inner join snwd_so as so	
10 on bp.client = so.client	
11 and bp.node_key = so.buyer_guid	
12 where bp.client = :im_client	Input Pane
13 group by bp.bp_id	
14 order by sum(so.gross_amount) desc;	
15	▲ ⬡ Input Parameters
16	IM_CLIENT
17 END;	IM_NUMBER
18 /********* End Procedure Script ***********/	

Consumed the above Stored Procedure in the following ABAP Report:

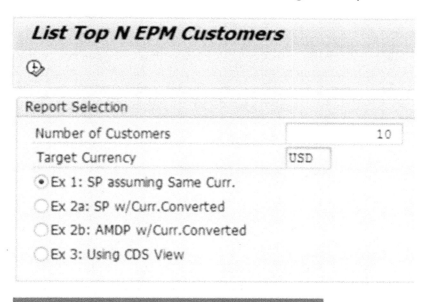

List Top N EPM Customers

Report Selection

Number of Customers		10
Target Currency	USD	

- ⦿ Ex 1: SP assuming Same Curr.
- ◯ Ex 2a: SP w/Curr.Converted
- ◯ Ex 2b: AMDP w/Curr.Converted
- ◯ Ex 3: Using CDS View

Output

Exercise 1: Assuming Same Currency

BP_ID	GROSS_AMOUNT
0100000026	262386.63
0100000000	254707.59
0100000024	133951.23
0100000006	133951.23
0100000008	105340.02
0100000021	105340.02
0100000022	75546.07
0100000005	75546.07
0100000023	46677.27
0100000003	46677.27

Exercise 2a: Create and Consume Stored Procedure with Currency Conversion

Requirement:

In Ex-1 don't assume the currency values are same. In the Stored Procedure take another input parameter as target currency and list out the Top N BP & Gross Order Value converted in target currency (in descending order)

Solution:

Created the following Stored Procedure:

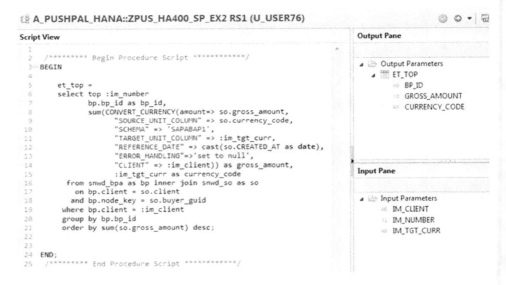

Consumed the above Stored Procedure in the following ABAP Report:

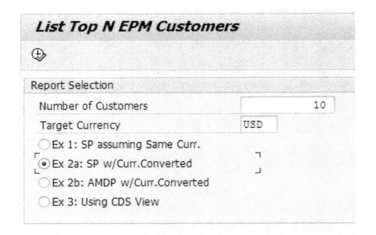

⌐ Output

Exercise 2: With Currency Conversion

BP_ID	GROSS_AMOUNT	CURRENCY_CODE
0100000026	246643.43	USD
0100000000	239425.13	USD
0100000024	125914.15	USD
0100000006	125914.15	USD
0100000008	99019.61	USD
0100000021	99019.61	USD
0100000022	71013.3	USD
0100000005	71013.3	USD
0100000023	43876.63	USD
0100000003	43876.63	USD

Refer to Source Code at end of this file.

Exercise 2b: Create and consume AMDP with Currency_Conversion

Requirement:

In Ex-2a we have solved it using a Stored Procedure. Now create a AMDP Method which will return the BP & Sum of Gross Sales Values converted to a Target Currency.

From a ABAP program call this AMDP Method to list out the top N customers.

Categorize the customers as below:

Gross Sales Value > 200000 then High

Between 100000 & 200000 then Medium

< 100000 then Low

Solution:

Created the following AMDP Class (in ADT):

CLASS zpus_ha400_cl_amdp_ex3 DEFINITION

   PUBLIC

   FINAL

   CREATE PUBLIC .

PUBLIC SECTION.

   interfaces if_amdp_marker_hdb.

```
* Structure for Results
TYPES: BEGIN OF ly_cust_ex3,
                 bp_id                    TYPE snwd_partner_id,
                 gross_amount             TYPE snwd_ttl_gross_amount,
                 currency_code            TYPE snwd_curr_code,
                 custtype                 TYPE char6,
          END OF ly_cust_ex3.

* Table Type for Results
   types ly_t_cust_ex3 TYPE STANDARD TABLE OF ly_cust_ex3.


* AMDP Method to Retrieve Top N EPM Customers
methods    METH_GET_TOP         value(IM_MANDT)        type mandt
           importing
                                value(IM_NUMBER)       type    i
                                value(IM_TGT_CURR) type snwd_curr_code
           exporting            value(ET_TOP_CUST) type ly_t_cust_ex3.
PROTECTED  SECTION.
PRIVATE SECTION.
ENDCLASS.


CLASS zpus_ha400_cl_amdp_ex3 IMPLEMENTATION.
method METH_GET_TOP by atabase PROCEDURE FOR HDB
                LANGUAGE SQLSCRIPT
                options READ-ONLY
                using snwd_bpa snwd_so.
lt_cust_usd =
select top :im_number
    bp.bp_id as bp_id,
    sum(convert_currency(amount => so.gross_amount,
            "SOURCE_UNIT_COLUMN" => so.currency_code,
            "SCHEMA" => 'SAPABAP1',
            "TARGET_UNIT_COLUMN" => :im_tgt_curr,
```

```
            "REFERENCE_DATE" => cast(so.CREATED_AT as date),

            "ERROR_HANDLING"=>'set to null',
                            "CLIENT" => :im_mandt)
    ) as gross_amount,
:im_tgt_curr as currency_code
from snwd_bpa as bp inner join snwd_so as so
    on bp.client = so.client and
            bp.node_key = so.buyer_guid
where bp.client = :im_mandt
group by bp.bp_id
order by gross_amount desc;
ET_TOP_CUST =
select bp_id,
    gross_amount,
    currency_code,
    case
            WHEN gross_amount > 200000 THEN 'High'
            WHEN gross_amount BETWEEN 100000 AND 200000 THEN
            'Medium' ELSE 'Low'
end as custtype
from :lt_cust_usd;
endmethod.
ENDCLASS.
```

Called the above AMDP Class-Method in the following ABAP Report:

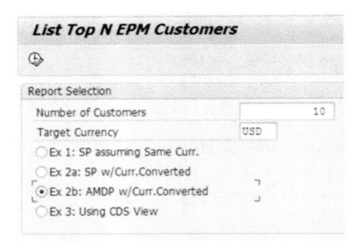

Refer to Source Code at end of this file.

Exercise 3: Create and Consume CDS View without Currency Conversion

Requirement:

In Ex-1 we have solved it using an AMDP. Now create a CDS view which will return the BP & Sum of Gross Sales Values.

From a ABAP program call this CDS view and using new Open SQL list out the top N customers.

Categorize the customers as below:

Gross Sales Value > 200000 then High

Between 100000 & 200000 then Medium

< 100000 then Low

Solution:

Created the following CDS View:

```
[RS1] ZPUS_HA400_CDS_EX3
 1  @AbapCatalog.sqlViewName: 'ZPUS_CDS_EX3'
 2  @ClientDependent: true
 3  @AbapCatalog.compiler.CompareFilter: true
 4  @AccessControl.authorizationCheck: #CHECK
 5  @EndUserText.label: 'CDS View to find Top N EPM Customers'
 6  define view Zpus_Ha400_Cds_Ex3
 7      with parameters im_client : MANDT
 8  as select from snwd_so as so inner join snwd_bpa as bp
 9  on bp.client = so.client and
10      bp.node_key = so.buyer_guid
11  {
12      bp.bp_id as bp_id,
13      sum(so.gross_amount) as gross_amount,
14      so.currency_code as currency_code
15  }
16  where so.client = :im_client
17  group by bp.bp_id, so.currency_code;
18
```

Consumed the above CDS in the following ABAP Report:

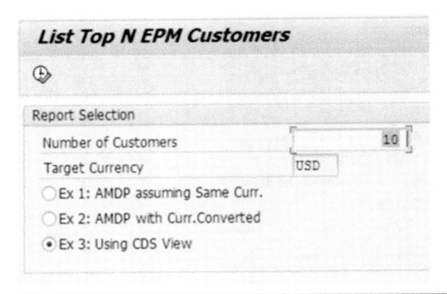

Exercise 3: CDS View with Customer Classification

BP_ID	GROSS_AMOUNT	CURRENCY_CODE	CUSTTYPE
0100000026	262386.63	EUR	High
0100000000	254707.59	EUR	High
0100000006	133951.23	EUR	Medium
0100000024	133951.23	EUR	Medium
0100000008	105340.02	EUR	Medium
0100000021	105340.02	EUR	Medium
0100000005	75546.07	EUR	Low
0100000022	75546.07	EUR	Low
0100000003	46677.27	EUR	Low
0100000023	46677.27	EUR	Low

Refer to Source Code at end of this file.

Exercise 4: Fuzzy and Type Ahead help in Selection-screen

Requirement:

Create a search help in ABAP data dictionary for Business Partner. Table for Selection is SNWD_BPA Search help should have type features for proposal for input fields. It should have fuzzy capability

User can search BP by BP Id, Company Name, Email Address or Phone Number

Add this search help in an ABAP report and test.

Solution:

Created the following Search Help:

Dictionary: Change Search Help

Elementary srch hlp	ZPUS_HA400_SH_EX4	Active
Short description	Search Help for HA400 Exercise 4	

Attributes / Definition

Data Collection

Selection method	SNWD_BPA
Text table	

Dialog Behavior

Dialog type	Display values immediately
Hot key	

Enhanced Options

☑ Proposal Search for Input Fields
☑ Full Text Fuzzy Search (Database-Specific)
Accuracy Value for Error-Tolerant Full Text Search 0,7

Search help exit

Parameter

Search help parameter	IMP	EXP	LPos	SPos	SDis	Data element	M...	Defaul
BP_ID	☑	☑	1	1	☐	SNWD_PARTNER_ID	☐	
COMPANY_NAME	☑	☐	2		☐	SNWD_COMPANY_NAME	☐	
EMAIL_ADDRESS	☑	☐	3		☐	SNWD_EMAIL_ADDRESS	☐	
PHONE_NUMBER	☑	☐	4		☐	SNWD_PHONE_NUMBER	☐	
	☐	☐			☐		☐	

Implemented the above Search Help in the Selection-screen of a sample program as follows:

Type any search string (say "Techn")

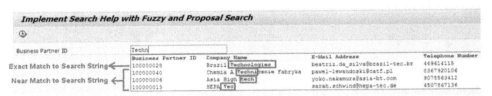

Select the last record.

Given below is the source-code extract for all the first 3 exercises above:

REPORT zpus_ha400_ex1.

* Selection screen

SELECTION-SCREEN BEGIN OF BLOCK cus WITH FRAME TITLE text-t01.

PARAMETERS: p_num TYPE i DEFAULT 10,

                p_tgt TYPE snwd_curr_code DEFAULT 'USD',

                p_ex1 TYPE xfeld RADIOBUTTON GROUP ex USER-COMMAND abcd, p_ex2a TYPE xfeld RADIOBUTTON GROUP ex,

                p_ex2b TYPE xfeld RADIOBUTTON GROUP ex DEFAULT 'X', p_ex3 TYPE xfeld RADIOBUTTON GROUP ex.

SELECTION-SCREEN END OF BLOCK cus.

AT SELECTION-SCREEN OUTPUT.

  LOOP AT SCREEN INTO screen.

```
IF screen-name CS 'P_TGT'.
IF p_ex2a = abap_true OR
          p_ex2b = abap_true.
        screen-input = 1.
     ELSE.
        screen-input = 0.
     ENDIF.
   ENDIF.
   MODIFY screen FROM screen.
 ENDLOOP.
START-OF-SELECTION.
CASE abap_true.
WHEN p_ex1.
     * Exercise 1: Consume Stored Procedure assuming same currency
     PERFORM sub_get_data_ex1 USING p_num.
   WHEN p_ex2a.
* Exercise 2a: Consume Stored Procedure with Currency Conversion
     PERFORM sub_get_data_ex2a USING p_num

                                p_tgt.
   WHEN p_ex2b.
     * Exercise 2b: Consume AMDP with Currency Conversion and Customer
     Classification
     PERFORM sub_get_data_ex2b USING p_num

                                p_tgt.
   WHEN p_ex3.
     * Exercise 3: Consume CDS View with Customer Classification PERFORM
     sub_get_data_ex3 USING p_num.
 ENDCASE.
*&------------------------------------------------------------------*
*&       Form   SUB_GET_DATA_EX1
*&------------------------------------------------------------------* FORM sub_get_data_
ex1 USING uv_number TYPE i.
```

```
* Structure for Results
TYPES: BEGIN OF ly_cust_ex1,
            bp_id               TYPE snwd_partner_id,
            gross_amount    TYPE snwd_ttl_gross_amount,
            END OF ly_cust_ex1.
DATA lt_cust_ex1 TYPE STANDARD TABLE OF ly_cust_ex1.
* Declarations for result overview TYPES: BEGIN OF ly_overview,
            param TYPE string, value TYPE string,
            END OF ly_overview.
DATA lt_overview TYPE STANDARD TABLE OF ly_overview. FIELD-SYMBOLS
<lfs_overview> TYPE ly_overview.
TRY.
* Create statement object (primary DB connection) DATA(lo_sql) = NEW cl_
sql_statement( ).
```

```
* Call Procedure with Overview (fill lt_overview)
    DATA(lo_result) = lo_sql->execute_query(
```

```
                    |CALL "_SYS_BIC"."A_PUSHPAL_HANA/ZPUS_
                    HA400_SP_EX1"( | && |{ sy-mandt }, { uv_number
                    }, null ) WITH OVERVIEW | ).
```

```
    lo_result->set_param_table( REF #( lt_overview ) ).
    lo_result->next_package( ).
    lo_result->close( ).
```

```
* Retrieve first result (Parameter et_early)
```

```
                    READ TABLE lt_overview ASSIGNING <lfs_overview> WITH
                            KEY param = 'ET_TOP'.
    lo_result = lo_sql->execute_query( |SELECT * FROM { <lfs_overview>-
    value } | ). lo_result->set_param_table( REF #( lt_cust_ex1 ) ). lo_result-
    >next_package( ).
    lo_result->close( ).
```

```
*   Exception handling
        CATCH cx_sql_exception INTO DATA(lo_sql_exc). "Excpt. Class for SQL
        Error MESSAGE lo_sql_exc TYPE 'I'.
        LEAVE LIST-PROCESSING.
    ENDTRY.
*   Display Output
    IF NOT lt_cust_ex1 IS INITIAL.
        cl_demo_output =>display_data( value = lt_cust_ex1

                                           name  = 'Exercise 1: Assuming Same
                                           Currency' ).
    ENDIF.
ENDFORM. " SUB_GET_DATA_EX1
*&---------------------------------------------------------------------*
*&        Form    SUB_GET_DATA_EX2A
*&---------------------------------------------------------------------*
FORM sub_get_data_ex2a USING uv_number     TYPE i
                              uv_tgt_curr TYPE snwd_curr_code.


*   Structure for Results
    TYPES: BEGIN OF ly_cust_ex2,
                bp_id              TYPE snwd_partner_id,
                gross_amount       TYPE snwd_ttl_gross_amount,
                currency_code      TYPE snwd_curr_code,
            END OF ly_cust_ex2.
    DATA lt_cust_ex2 TYPE STANDARD TABLE OF ly_cust_ex2.
*   Declarations for result overview TYPES: BEGIN OF ly_overview,
                param TYPE string, value TYPE string,
            END OF ly_overview.
    DATA lt_overview TYPE STANDARD TABLE OF ly_overview. FIELD-SYMBOLS
    <lfs_overview> TYPE ly_overview.
    TRY.
*   Create statement object (primary DB connection) DATA(lo_sql) = NEW
    cl_sql_statement( ).
```

```
            * Call Procedure with Overview (fill lt_overview)
            DATA(lo_result) = lo_sql->execute_query(
                                |CALL "_SYS_BIC"."A_PUSHPAL_HANA/ZPUS_
                                HA400_SP_EX2"( | &&

                                |{ sy-mandt }, { uv_number }, '{ uv_tgt_curr }', null )
                                WITH OVERVIEW | ).

         lo_result->set_param_table( REF #( lt_overview ) ).

         lo_result->next_package( ).

         lo_result->close( ).

          * Retrieve first result (Parameter et_early)
                        READ TABLE lt_overview ASSIGNING <lfs_overview> WITH
                                    KEY param = 'ET_TOP'.

         lo_result = lo_sql->execute_query( |SELECT * FROM { <lfs_overview>-
         value } | ). lo_result->set_param_table( REF #( lt_cust_ex2 ) ). lo_result-
         >next_package( ).

         lo_result->close( ).

      *   Exception handling
          CATCH cx_sql_exception INTO DATA(lo_sql_exc). "Excpt. Class for SQL
          Error MESSAGE lo_sql_exc TYPE 'I'.

          LEAVE LIST-PROCESSING.

   ENDTRY.

   *      Display Output
         IF NOT lt_cust_ex2 IS INITIAL. cl_demo_output=>display_data( value =
         lt_cust_ex2

                                    name  = 'Exercise 2: With Currency
                                    Conversion' ).

      ENDIF.
ENDFORM. " SUB_GET_DATA_EX2A
*&---------------------------------------------------------------------*
*&         Form    SUB_GET_DATA_EX2B
*&---------------------------------------------------------------------*
FORM sub_get_data_ex2b USING uv_number      TYPE i
                              uv_tgt_curr TYPE snwd_curr_code.
```

```
*  Structure for Results
   TYPES: BEGIN OF ly_cust_ex3,
                bp_id               TYPE snwd_partner_id,
                gross_amount        TYPE snwd_ttl_gross_amount,
                currency_code       TYPE snwd_curr_code,
                custtype            TYPE char6,
          END OF ly_cust_ex3.
          DATA lt_cust_ex2b TYPE zpus_ha400_cl_amdp_ex3=>ly_t_cust_ex3.
*  Call AMDP Method get to EPM Customers
*    DATA(lo_object) = NEW zpus_ha400_cl_amdp_ex3( ).
NEW zpus_ha400_cl_amdp_ex3(      )->meth_get_top( EXPORTING im_mandt
                                 = sy-mandt im_number = uv_number
                                 im_tgt_curr = uv_tgt_curr

                          IMPORTING et_top_cust = lt_cust_ex2b ).
*  Display Output
   IF NOT lt_cust_ex2b IS INITIAL. cl_demo_output=>display_data( value =
      lt_cust_ex2b


                          name  = 'Exercise 2b: AMDP View with
                          Customer Classification'
).
   ENDIF.
ENDFORM. " SUB_GET_DATA_EX3
*&---------------------------------------------------------------------*
*&      Form    SUB_GET_DATA_EX3
*&---------------------------------------------------------------------*
FORM sub_get_data_ex3 USING uv_number TYPE i.
*  Structure for Results
   TYPES: BEGIN OF ly_cust_ex3,
                bp_id               TYPE snwd_partner_id,
                gross_amount        TYPE snwd_ttl_gross_amount,
                currency_code       TYPE snwd_curr_code,
                custtype            TYPE char6,
```

```
        END OF ly_cust_ex3.
   DATA lt_cust_ex3 TYPE STANDARD TABLE OF ly_cust_ex3.
*  Check if Feature is Supported or not IF cl_abap_dbfeatures=>use_features(
                        EXPORTING
                        requested_features = VALUE #( (
cl_abap_dbfeatures=>views_with_parameters ) )
                        ).
*     Consume CDS View SELECT bp_id,
           gross_amount, currency_code,
           CASE WHEN gross_amount > 200000 THEN 'High'
                WHEN gross_amount BETWEEN 100000 AND 200000 THEN
                'Medium'
                ELSE 'Low'
           END AS custtype
        UP TO @uv_number ROWS
      FROM zpus_ha400_cds_ex3( im_client = @sy-mandt )
      INTO TABLE @lt_cust_ex3
      ORDER BY gross_amount DESCENDING.
*     Display Output
      IF NOT lt_cust_ex3 IS INITIAL. cl_demo_output=>display_data( value =
         lt_cust_ex3
name                                                      = 'Exercise 3:
                                  CDS View with Customer Classification'
).
      ENDIF.
    ELSE.
      MESSAGE i398(00) WITH 'Consuming External Views with Parameters is not
      supported'.
      LEAVE LIST-PROCESSING.
    ENDIF.
  ENDIF.
ENDFORM. " SUB_GET_DATA_EX3
```

6.13 SAP Fiori Cloud for S/4HANA - Implementation Quick Guide

* Quick Guide for Implementation: Internal Access Point

The following procedure guides you through the process of setting up SAP Fiori Cloud in an internal access point scenario.

This implementation quick guide contains the basic information required for the respective steps with links to more detailed information, such as the underlying concepts in the landscape configuration guide or more detailed step-by-step procedures in the respective product documentation. We recommend that you right-click on these links and choose *Open Link in New Tab* (Google Chrome) or *Open in New Tab* (Internet Explorer). Otherwise, going back to this guide may be cumbersome and you easily loose track where you are.

The following figure depicts the system landcsape for the internal access point scenario.

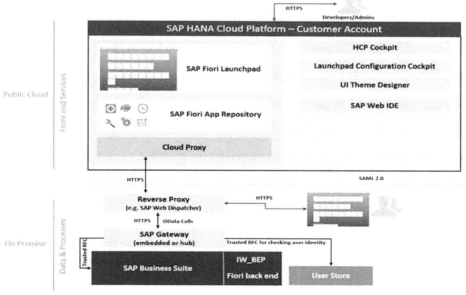

Figure 1: Internal Access Point Landscape

Internal Access Point Landscape

Prerequisites

When you log on to SAP HANA Cloud Platform for the first time after subscribing to SAP Fiori Cloud, you are subscribed to the portal service, but no other subscriptions or content is available.

To activate the subscriptions for your account, open the *Services* panel in your SAP HANA Cloud Platform

account, choose ▶ *Portal Service* ▶ *Go to Service*. A cloud portal site directory opens where you create a new launchpad site. The SAP Fiori launchpad configuration cockpit (FCC) opens and a popup is displayed. In the popup, select *SAP Fiori Cloud for S/4HANA* and choose *Add Content*. If you skip the popup, you can access it back by choosing *Add Content to Launchpad* from the user menu in the upper right corner.

Once you have selected the content, the popup no longer appears when you open the FCC and the entry in the user menu disappears. Your content and subscriptions will then be available in your account and you can start with the implementation.

Your choice is account-specific: If you create a new account on SAP HANA Cloud Platform, the dialog appears again when you log on to FCC the first time.

Step 1: Select the SAP Fiori Apps for SAP Fiori Cloud

Currently, SAP Fiori Cloud provides an extract of the available SAP Fiori apps. Whereas the front end components for the SAP Fiori apps for SAP Fiori Cloud are provided by the SAP HANA Cloud Platform, you have to make sure that the required back end components are available in your back end system.

The SAP Fiori apps reference library contains information about the product features as well as information about the required back end components, versions, and support packages for each app and enables you to decide about the apps you want to implement.

To access the SAP Fiori apps reference library and to send the information about the back end requirements to the system administrator, proceed as follows:

* Open the SAP Fiori apps reference library under https://fioriappslibrary. hana.ondemand.com and select the *Available via SAP Fiori Cloud* category on the left hand side.

* From the list of available apps, select the apps that you want to implement:

To create a holistic view of the required implementation and configuration steps, choose *Aggregate*.

To share this information with the system administrator who has to make sure that all required back end requirements are met, choose *Share*.

The system administrator needs this information later in the process for setting up the back end system and the connection to the SAP HANA Cloud Platform.

Step 2: Set Up Your SAP HANA Cloud Platform Account

Your account on SAP HANA Cloud Platform is your single point of access to all services for configuring the cloud-side of SAP Fiori Cloud. When you sign up for SAP Fiori Cloud, your account on the SAP HANA Cloud Platform is

provided to you, fully provisioned with the required services. The account information that you need for initial logon is provided in the e-mail you receive after you have signed up for SAP Fiori Cloud.

Log on to SAP HANA Cloud Platform. On the overview page, you can:

* Create additional accounts for your organization.

* Manage the quota.

* Create integration tokens.

When you open your *Account*, all services you require for setting up and configuring SAP Fiori Cloud are described in the following steps are available in the panel on the left hand side.

Step 3: Assign SAP HANA Cloud Platform Member Roles

Members can access accounts and use the SAP HANA Cloud Platform cockpit based on their assigned roles. The roles define the scope of the available functionality the user can access.

When you subscribe to SAP Fiori Cloud, the initial account information is a part of the sales order and contains the HCP access data for the *Administrator* member role. We recommend to create at least two more administrators immediately after you receive the initial account information. This avoids roadblocks in the implementation due to an unavailability of the HCP access data. Alternatively, if you do not have access to the initial account information, open a ticket to get another user with *Administrator* role added.

Prerequisites:

● You have a user with *Administrator* role for your HCP account.

● The members you want to add have a SAP user ID. The user IDs can be requested on SAP Service Marketplace under http://service.sap.com/request-user. These users are automatically registered with the SAP ID service, which controls user access to SAP HANA Cloud Platform.

To add account members and assign roles, open the *Members* panel in the SAP HANA Cloud Platform cockpit and choose *Add Members*. Enter the user IDs and select the respective roles.

Step 4: Install, Configure, and Activate SAP Gateway (On-Premise Installation Only)

You use the SAP Gateway to set up and activate the OData services which retrieve the business data for the SAP Fiori apps from your back end system.

Prerequisites: If no SAP Gateway is installed yet, choose one of the deployment options for SAP Gateway and install the SAP Gateway components accordingly.

The following steps only give a rough overview about the mandatory and optional configuration tasks. For configuring and activating the SAP Gateway, use the SAP Gateway Configuration Guide.

- Make the general configuration settings (mandatory).
- Configure the OData channels (mandatory).
- Configure the settings for content scenarios (optional).

Step 5: Install Back End OData Components

Based on the aggregated information from the SAP Fiori apps reference library, the system administrator installs all required back end components and applies the required notes.

The steps below describe the general process that we recommend.

Proceed as follows:

- To plan the additions to your on-premise system and to download the corresponding software components, use the Maintenance Planner. You can choose *Prepare apps for planning with Maintenance Planner* in the SAP Fiori apps reference library, however, we strongly recommend to call the Maintenance Planner directly.

- Use the Software Provisioning Manager for the installation of new components or the Software Update Manager for updates of the existing components for the installation in your on-premise system.

Both tools are available on the SAP Service Marketplace as part of the Software Logistics Toolset.

In addition to the components, it may be necessary to install SAP notes. The required notes are mentioned in the SAP Fiori apps reference library, however, we recommend that you perform a search in SAP notes.

Step 6: Assign Back End Authorization Roles

Back end authorization roles are provided for the OData services. These roles need to be assigned to users. The role information is available in the aggregated information in the SAP Fiori app reference library under

Aggregated Configuration Information ⟩ *Back-End Authorization Roles (PFCG)* ⟩.

To assign the roles to users, proceed as follows:

1. Open transaction PFCG in the back end system and enter the role name.

   *Open the *User* tab and enter the User IDs.

   *Save your entries.

Step 7: Register, Confirm, and Test OData

SAP Fiori uses OData as protocol for the communication with the back end system. OData is a RESTful protocol, leveraging HTTP GET/POST/PUT methods. The OData services are provided by the SAP Gateway server or the OData provisioning service on HCP.

You find the required OData service names in the *Aggregated Configuration Requirements* section of the aggregated app information from the SAP Fiori app reference library. Go to the *OData Services* section and note the OData services and versions you need.

To register the OData services in the SAP Gateway system, proceed as follows:

* Assign OData service authorizations in SAP Gateway.

In the SAP Gateway system, assign the OData service authorization to a new or existing role, such as a business role that has been adjusted according to your needs. Proceed as follows:

In transaction PFCG create the role Z_GW_USER with the authorization profiles / IWFND/RT_GW_USER and S_SERVICE. Assign this role to your Fiori user and Fiori admin user.

In transaction PFCG create the role Z_GW_ADMIN with the authorization profile / IWFND/RT_ADMIN. Assign this role to your Fiori admin user.

* Open transaction /IWFND/MAiNT_SERVICE and choose *Get Services* or filter for

specific service.

* Select the service and add the selected services.

* On the *Activate and Maintain Services* page, double check that your services have been added to the list of services.

* Select one of the OData services and choose ⏷ *SAP Gateway Client* ⏵ *Execute* ⏷. Check the response and test one of the collections.

Note

Instead of activating OData services individually for each app, use a task list to activate the OData services for several apps at the same time.

Step 8: Configure the SAP Fiori Apps in the Back End

Check in the back end configuration section of the aggregated information from the SAP Fiori apps reference library if configuration in the back end system is required for the apps.

Step 9: Configure the SAP Fiori Apps in the SAP Fiori Launchpad Configuration Cockpit

The SAP Fiori apps are now deployed to the SAP HANA Cloud Platform and you can start the configuration in the SAP Fiori launchpad configuration cockpit (FCC). You can access the FCC either from the SAP Fiori launchpad or from the *Services* panel of the SAP HANA Cloud Platform.

The required fields are preconfigured. You can adapt this configuration, if required.

Step 10: Set Up User Authentication and Principal Propagation

The user authentication establishes and verifies the identity of a user. This is a prerequisite for accessing the SAP Fiori apps. The apps are protected with a SAML 2.0 authentication method, authenticating the user against a trusted identity provider. This authentication method is used in combination with principal propagation through short-lived certificates to pass the user identity from the client.

Proceed as follows:

• Configure trust in the SAP HANA Cloud Connector.

• Configure the settings for SAML 2.0 communication between HCP and the trusted identity provider in the *Trust* panel of the HCP cockpit.

• Establish trust between HCP and your corporate IdP.

- Establish trust on the level of your corporate IdP to the service provider on HCP.

Establish user propagation by means of the *PrincipalPropagation* property in the *Destinations* panel of the HCP cockpit.

- Connect to the user store. If you have an existing on-premise system with a populated user store, you can connect SAP HANA Cloud Platform to use this on-premise user store via the SAP Cloud Identity service. This connection is used to check credentials, search for users, retrieve user details, and retrieve information about the groups a user is a member of, which can then be used for authorization.

Step 11: Set Up Authorization Flow

You define the authorization flow by means of users, roles and user groups which you assign to application roles and catalogs.

Assigning Cloud Portal Roles to User Groups and Users

First, you assign SAP Fiori launchpad on cloud users to business roles and define groups. Open the Portal service in the HCP Cockpit and choose *Configure Portal Services Roles*. Here you can create new roles and groups and assign users to roles and groups.

The TENANT_ADMIN role is predefined to your user. Assign this role to other users who shall have administrative permissions over the launchpad, and access the SAP Fiori configuration cockpit (FCC). You can assign the role to single users or you can define a group for users with admin rights and assign the role to the group.

Assign Content to Roles

** Assign end users to a user group by means of SAML 2.0 assertions.

SAML 2.0 assertions can be used to transfer user attributes from an identity provider (IdP) to a service provider. The attributes can be specified on IdP level and may also be used to transfer information about user groups. The IdP may have a custom configuration concerning which user groups are to be included into the target assertion. The way the attributes are transferred is standardizes and based on SAML 2.0 specification. On the service provider side, a user can be mapped automatically to user groups based on the attribute valies. The user groups must be created manually by the customer's administrator.

- Define the application roles.

Open the *Subscriptions* panel in the HCP cockpit and choose one of your subscribed apps. Open the *Roles* panel and create the required roles for the app. These roles should be associated with the target business scenarios that are available for your end users.

Assign user groups to the app roles.

You can assign user groups to the app roles either in the *Roles* panel of the *Subscriptions* panel in the HCP cockpit, or on the *Authorizations* panel.

- Include the app role in a catalog.

You use catalogs for application role assignment. A content admin has to add the application roles to the correpsonding catalogs. All users assigned to the application role via the user group can access the content of the catalogs that are also assigned to this application role. This means that all users assigned to a certain user group in a target IdP or LDAP system have access to all application roles in the corresponding catalog.

To assign the app role to catalogs, open the SAP Fiori configuration cockpit and select *Catalogs*.

Step 12: Set Up and Configure the Reverse Proxy

A reverse proxy loads the UI components from the SAP HANA Cloud Platform while the OData calls remain in the customer's network. The reverse proxy is installed and running in the on premise landscape. You can, for example, use the SAP Web Dispatcher as reverse proxy for SAP Fiori Cloud.

The SAML2 identity provider is configured in HCP as described in *Step 11: Set up Authorization Flow*.

The SAML2 identity provider is configured in the same ABAP AS in which the SAP Gateway is running.

Note

In the SAML2 IdP service provider configuration, all end points to the SAP Gateway should have the reverse proxy host name. For example, if the gateway host name is my-sap-gateway.internal.corp and the reverse proxy host name is my-reverse-proxy.internal.corp, for the assertion consumer service endpoint https://my-sap-gateway.internal.corp/sap/saml2/sp/acs/000 should be replaced with https://my-reverse-proxy.internal.corp/sap/saml2/sp/acs/000.

Note

Blocking third-party cookies in your web browser can cause problems in the authentication flow between the

SAP Fiori launchpad and the Gateway system. To avoid this, apply one of the following options:

- Run the SAML2 IdP and the reverse proxy on the same domain.

- Enable third-party cookies in the web browser.

- If third-party cookies shall be disabled, add an exception for the SAML2 IdP domain; note that this option is not applicable in mobile devices.

Apply the SAP notes 1977537 and 2193513 to your SAP Gateway system if they do not already exist in your installed support package.

To set up SAP Fiori launchpad and SAP Gateway access for the internal internal access point scenario, you need to set up and configure the reverse proxy:

Note

The configuration examples in the following procedure are using the SAP Web Dispatcher as an example for reverse proxy configuration. However, you can use any standard reverse proxy as well.

1. The reverse proxy accesses the SAP Fiori launchpad with a preconfigured custom domain.

Note

Before you start with the configuration, you need to have a quota for domains configured for your account,

Proceed as follows:

- Install the SDK tool.

- Follow the custom domain configuration.

Note

In the following steps, mycustomdomain.com is used as custom domain and my-reverse-proxy.internal.corp is used as reverse proxy domain.

- Add the routes to SAP Fiori launchpad (FLP) on cloud and to the SAP Gateway system in the configuration file for reverse proxy properties.

Note

The port for the SAP Fiori launchpad and SAP Gateway routes shall be the default SSL port – 443.

- Route to FLP on cloud:

The URL paths that start with the following paths should be routed to your SAP Fiori launchpad on custom domain (mycustomdomain.com) after each route: / cloud/flp /sites /sap/

fiori /sap/bc/lrep /saml2 /fiori /v1 /portal /flp /themedesigner /api /orion / resources/sap/dfa/help /sap/ui5/1/resources/sap/dfa/help /sap/ui5/1/ innovation/ resources/sap/dfa/help /sap/ui5/1/fcc/resources/sap/dfa/help /sap/ dfa/

help /sap/bc/ui2/app_index /sap/backend/

Example

Example: Routes from SAP Web Dispatcher to FLP on cloud:

- SID = unique system ID, for example FLP
- EXTSRV = mycustomdomain.com (custom domain as defined in step 1)
- SRCSRC = 443 (default SSL port)
- SRCURL = /cloud/flp;/sites;/sap/fiori;/sap/bc/lrep;/saml2;/fiori;/v1;/ portal;/flp;/themedesigner;/api;/orion;/resources/sap/dfa/help;/sap/ ui5/1/ resources/sap/dfa/help;/sap/ui5/1/innovation/resources/sap/dfa/ help;/sap/ ui5/1/fcc/resources/sap/dfa/help;/sap/dfa/help;/sap/bc/ui2/ app_index;/sap/ backend
- PROXY = Customer network proxy
- Additional settings: STANDARD_COOKIE_FILTER = OFF, SSL_ENCRYPT = 2

wdisp/system_8 = SID=FLP, EXTSRV=https://mycustomdomain.com:443, SCRSRV=*: 443, SRCURL=/cloud/flp;/sites;/sap/fiori;/sap/bc/lrep;/saml2;/fiori;/ v1;/ portal;/flp;/themedesigner;/api;/orion;/resources/sap/dfa/help;/sap/ ui5/1/ resources/sap/dfa/help;/sap/ui5/1/innovation/resources/sap/dfa/help;/ sap/ ui5/1/fcc/resources/sap/dfa/help;/sap/dfa/help;/sap/bc/ui2/app_index;/ sap/ backend, PROXY=<customer's proxy>, STANDARD_COOKIE_FILTER=OFF, SSL_ENCRYPT=2

- Route to SAP Gateway system:

The URL paths that start with the following paths should be routed to your SAP Gateway system (my-sap-gateway.internal.corp) after the routes: /sap/opu/odata

/sap/saml2.

Example

Example: Routes to the SAP Gateway system:

* SID = SAP system ID, for example XYZ

* NR = SAP system number

* CLIENT = SAP system client

* MSHOST = Message server host

* MSPORT = Message server port

* SRCSRV = 443 (default SSL port)

* SRCURL = SAP Gateway OData (/sap/opu/odata) and SAML2 paths (/sap/saml2)

* Additional settings: STANDARD_COOKIE_FILTER = OFF

wdisp/system_1 = SID=<SAP system ID>, NR=<nr>, CLIENT=<client number>, MSHOST=<MS host>, MSPORT=<MS port>, SCRSRV=*:443, SRCURL=/sap/opu/odata;/sap/saml2, STANDARD_COOKIE_FILTER=OFF

- Enable the port in the reverse proxy for SAP Fiori Cloud routes.

Example

For SAP Web Dispatcher, enable port 443:

* PROT = Transfer protocol, HTTPS

* HOST = SAP Web Dispatcher host name

* PORT = Default SSL port

* EXTBIND =

icm/server_port_1 =

PROT=HTTPS,HOST=mywebdispatcher.zdm.corp,PORT=443,EXTBIND=1

- All routes that the reverse proxy forwards to the SAP Fiori launchpad (mycustomdomain.com) should be updated with the following headers:

HOST: Reverse proxy host (my-reverse-proxy.internal.corp)

X-Custom-Host: SAP Fiori launchpad custom domain (mycustomdomain.com)

Example

In SAP Web Dispatcher configuration, add a condition for SID=FLP in the redirect configuration file and add the X-Custom-Header to the request to FLP specifying the custom FLP domain. In the response, the FLP subscription URL in the location header should be overridden with the SAP Web Dispatcher URL.

if %{SID} = FLP

begin

SetHeader X-Custom-Host mycustomdomain.com

SetHeader HOST mywebdispatcher.zdm.corp

NOP {break}

end

- Upload the custom domain SSL certificate to the SAP Web Dispatcher (only required if you use SAP Web Dispatcher as reverse proxy).

Open the web dispatcher administration console and choose ⊩ *SSL and Trust Configuration* ❯ *PSE Management* ⌟. Choose the PSE file for your client certificates from the dropdown list. Unter *Trusted Certificates* choose *Import Certificate* and copy and paste the certificate including -----BEGIN CERTIFICATE----- and -----END CERTIFICATE-----. Choose *Import*.

(e) Optional, only relevant for SAP Web Dispatcher Configure the SAP Web Dispatcher to act as a global cache server.

This is an optional configuration that may help to improve the performance. To configure the global cache in the Web Dispatcher, add the following line to the Web Dispatcher's profile file: icm/HTTP/server_cache_0 = PREFIX=/

Step 13: Activate the Internal Access Point Scenario in FCC

In the SAP Fiori launchpad configuration cockpit, under ⇥ *Site Settings* ⟩ *Properties* ⟩ and switch to *Edit*. Select *Internal* then save and publish.

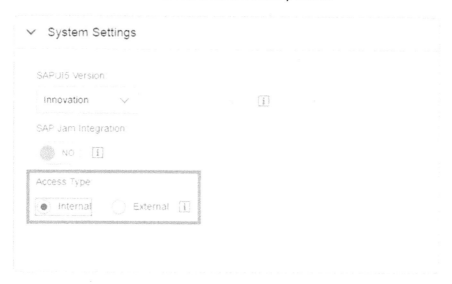

Step 14: Assign OData Service Authorizations

Assign OData service authorizations for the SAP Fiori apps to your users in SAP Gateway and on the back end server.

You need the following information for each SAP Fiori app:

* OData service (version number)

* Delivered authorization role (PFCG role) in the back end server

Caution

Several authorization default values are connected to the OData service. To ensure that all these default values are assigned to a user, follow the instructions in the documentation links provided below.

* Back end authorization roles are provided for the OData services. These roles need to be assigned to users. The role information is available in the aggregated information in the SAP Fiori app reference library under

⇥ *Aggregated Configuration Information* ⟩ *Back-End Authorization Roles (PFCG)* ⟩ . To assign the roles to users, proceed as follows:

In transaction PFCG, enter the role name according to the information in the SAP Fiori app library.

Note

Some roles provide an authorization template and not a role. In this case, create a custom role with the authorization template.

Open the *User* tab and enter the User IDs.

* Save your entries.

Note

To activate role assignments in the HCP, you need to refresh the session.

* Assign OData service authorizations in SAP Gateway.

In the SAP Gateway system, assign the OData service authorization to a new or existing role, such as a business role that has been adjusted according to your needs. Proceed as follows:

In transaction PFCG create the role Z_GW_USER with the authorization profiles / IWFND/RT_GW_USER and S_SERVICE. Assign this role to your Fiori user and Fiori admin user.

In transaction PFCG create the role Z_GW_ADMIN with the authorization profile / IWFND/RT_ADMIN. Assign this role to your Fiori admin user.

Step 15: Configure Single Log Out

To enable single logout, you need to configure the custom domain URLs for the SAML single sign-on flow in the HCP cockpit. Even if single sign-on works successfully with your application at the custom domain, you will need to follow the current procedure to enable single logout.

Proceed as follows:

* In the *Trust Settings* in HCP cockpit, open the *Custom Application Domains* tab.

* Enable *Use Custom Application Domains*. The *Central Redirect URL* field is preset.

* Enter your custom domain in the *Custom Domain URLs* field.

* Save your changes.

The system generates the respective single logout service endpoints. Test them in your Web browser and make sure they are accessible from there.

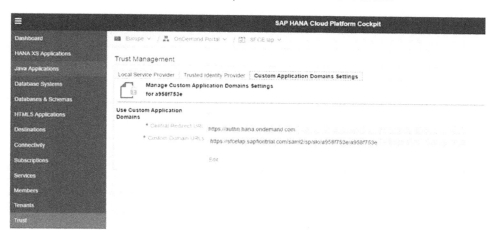

Important Disclaimers and Legal Information

Coding Samples

Any software coding and/or code lines / strings ("Code") included in this documentation are only examples and are not intended to be used in a productive system environment. The Code is only intended to better explain and visualize the syntax and phrasing rules of certain coding. SAP does not warrant the correctness and completeness of the Code given herein, and SAP shall not be liable for errors or damages caused by the usage of the Code, unless damages were caused by SAP intentionally or by SAP's gross negligence.

Accessibility

The information contained in the SAP documentation represents SAP's current view of accessibility criteria as of the date of publication; it is in no way intended to be a binding guideline on how to ensure accessibility of software products. SAP in particular disclaims any liability in relation to this document. This disclaimer, however, does not apply in cases of willful misconduct or gross negligence of SAP. Furthermore, this document does not result in any direct or indirect contractual obligations of SAP.

Gender-Neutral Language

As far as possible, SAP documentation is gender neutral. Depending on the context, the reader is addressed directly with "you", or a gender-neutral noun (such as "sales person" or "working days") is used. If when referring to members of both sexes, however, the third-person singular cannot be avoided or a gender-neutral noun does not exist, SAP reserves the right to use the masculine form of the noun and pronoun. This is to ensure that the documentation remains comprehensible.

Internet Hyperlinks

The SAP documentation may contain hyperlinks to the Internet. These hyperlinks are intended to serve as a hint about where to find related information. SAP does not warrant the availability and correctness of this related information or the ability of this information to serve a particular purpose. SAP shall not be liable for any damages caused by the use of related information unless damages have been caused by SAP's gross negligence or willful misconduct.

S/4 HANA Questionarie

What is the current SAP system landscape (ECC Enhancement Pack - ECC.60 EHP7, etc., Extensions - APO, etc.)

ECC EHP7 sp7

If ECC 6.0 EPH7, what were the results (transactions SPAU and SPDD) of the update in terms of standardization score, custom/problem objects, and testing?

In line with what we would expect with all of the customizations and development objects that we have. Recent EHP7 upgrade required extensive testing.

Last Upgrade

When was the last Upgrade?

July 2015 Upgrade to EHP7 from EHP5

Was there a full or partial integration test? One or multiple cycles of integration test before UAT?

Typically execute 3 rounds of functional integration testing (FIT).

UAT is typically conducted as part of FIT3 (sometimes FIT2 as well)

Automated regression testing typically occurs after FIT is complete prior to migrating to PRD

In the case of the last SAP upgrade, FITs were used for regression testing.

How Many Defects Logged

~100

Last Upgrade (continued)

How many months did the upgrade project last?

7 months

How many integration test cases are part of their regression testing suite?

We have a core set of about 50 regression tests that are executed after all integration testing is complete.

For the last SAP upgrade project we added many more via Panaya – probably hundreds.

What percentage of these are automated?

All regression testing is automated via our RR1 environment

How long does it take to execute full regression test suite and how many FTEs are needed?

Each FIT takes 2-3 weeks. Regression is completed in a manner of hours via automated scripts. Our migration/quality team oversees the regression testing.

How would you describe the SAP systems in terms of customization?

We do not modify core code, but we are highly customized in terms of custom developed tcodes, interfaces, user exits, smart forms, etc. We also have partners with name space areas within our development environment (i.e. SecurityWeaver, Taulia, etc.)

Has an Industry Solution been implemented?

No

How large is the database and on what DB and version is/are the system/s?

4.2 TB; Oracle DB v11.2.0.4 (will be upgraded to 12.1.0.2 by end of the year)

What is the length of time the system can be down for a system upgrade/ update?

60 hours over a weekend max (Friday 5pm to Monday 5am)

Is SAP Max Attention or similar SAP services in place?

We utilize [SAP Continuous Quality Check Service] CQC [services[when needed and also are now a [Customer COE (CCOE)] certified customer

*Continuous Quality Checks - Pilot Delivery

Data Consistency Management [PILOT]

Interface Management [PILOT]

*Continuous Quality Checks

Business Process Operations

Business Process Performance Optimization

Configuration Check

Data Volume Management

Downtime Assessment

EarlyWatch Check

Going Live Support

Implementation

Integration Validation

OS/DB Migration Check

Security Optimization

Technical Performance Optimization

Transport Execution Analysis

Upgrade, Upgrade Assessment

What are the top (3 - 5) Finance/month-end close related pain points the Finance organization has? Is there specific functionality that the Finance organization needs, but doesn't have?

Are there specific pain points in the materials planning or logistics areas? If so, what are 3 - 5? Is there specific functionality that the organization needs, but doesn't have?

How complex are the organization's inter-company activities? What percentage of sales transactions are inter-company? Is transfer pricing a core part of the company's business model?

Intercompany transactions are definitely part of the landscape at Hubbell. Specific pricing conditions and processes have been set up for this. Probably 5-10% of total sales are intercompany.

What are the top (5 - 10) background jobs and transactions in terms of longest to complete?

FICO:

WIP / Variance/Settlement monthly jobs

Product costing mass – structure explosion/costing

KE30 – COPA reports

KE24 COPA line items

SD:

BURNDYUS_V_V2

PROGRESS_V_V2

RACO_V_V2

BACKORDER

SD_C3_BILL_DUE

What are the top (5 - 10) background jobs and transactions in terms of longest to complete? (continued)

OPS:

MRP (RMMRP000)

HIT_DLY (RCPMAU01)

HPS_MPS_NET_CHG (RMMRP000)

MRP_CHANGE (RMMRP000)

FORECAST_REORG (RM60RR20)

What is the organization's typical risk profile? Bleeding edge implementer, Last to implement? Please describe.

Slightly above center

Is the organization poised to take on significant back office and/or change management projects in the near future?

Change is fairly standard in our culture

References

http://help.sap.com/hana/SAP_HANA_Developer_Guide_en.pdf

http://scn.sap.com/community/abap/eclipse/blog/2014/02/04/new-data-modeling-features-in-abap-for-hana

https://tutorialspoint.com

www.ingramcontent.com/pod-product-compliance
Lightning Source LLC
LaVergne TN
LVHW022307060326
832902LV00020B/3322